HIGHER

GROUND

DEEPER

TRUTH

ISBN: 978-0-8054-4385-1

Published by B & H Publishing Group,
Nashville, Tennessee

DEWEY: 248.3
SUBHEAD: CHRISTIAN LIFE \ PRAYER

15 14 13 12 11 10 9 8 7 6 5 4 3 2 1   10 09 08 07 06

HIGHER
GROUND
DEEPER
TRUTH

JIM & KAYE JOHNS

B&H
PUBLISHING GROUP

Nashville, Tennessee

To T. W. Hunt and Henry Blackaby

Our praise is to God alone; but our sincere prayer is that this book might be, from our hearts, an expression of our deep thanks to these two men through whose lives and words God first taught us to pray, and first revealed to us His path to higher ground. Their walk with God has been, and is today, our example. Their influence continues to shape our lives.

Contents

Definitions

We should explain what we mean by *Higher Ground* and *Deeper Truth.* Someone has said that if a title must be explained, you need a different title. Even though we feel that you probably have a good idea of what this book is about, we want to make it clear.

Higher Ground, as we intend it, speaks of personal spiritual growth, of *progress in our Christian life.* It is progress by steps, not by a single giant leap. So *Higher Ground* refers to upward, step-by-step movement toward a more intimate and fulfilling relationship with God.

Deeper Truth we will see as a growing *personal knowledge of God*—who He is, who we are in His eyes, and what that relationship is meant to be.

On both counts, the key is *relationship*—the experience of union with God in a person-to-person connection. This relationship is something that every true Christian desires (or, for some of us, desires to desire), but many struggle to understand and pursue. We who are born again do have the spark of the relationship because of the presence of the Holy Spirit within us. But the spark must be fanned into flame by our responses, our intentions, and our actions.

What we will see is that this relationship is founded upon and nurtured by prayer. What is needed first in many Christians' lives is simply a more practical and useful understanding of the part prayer plays in the process and how God has given instruction so that we may respond to His invitation. In other words, what do we need to know, and what are we to do? We need help if we are to enter and live in this relationship.

Toward that end, *Higher Ground, Deeper Truth* seeks to be a road map for a journey of discovery. On this journey, we find that each upward step is actually one leg of a longer trip. There are always more hills to climb, and Jesus has taken us by the hand to lead us on the journey. In that process, He reveals Himself while showing us more of what we ourselves are like now, as well as what we can become.

As we go, prayer will be our conversation with Him along the way. If we remain silent—prayerless—we will surely miss the help He gives to guide us. He has saved us, planted His own life in us, and stirred within us that desire to walk with Him. And He has committed Himself to hold us by the hand all the way.

Now let's move in step with the Savior—praying, listening, following as He leads. He knows the way to the higher ground, and He has deeper truth to share. We're on the journey together; we have the expectation of a dynamic and growing relationship with God in view; and we rejoice in anticipation of what lies ahead for all of us.

From Mystery to Maturity

For the Christian, mystery is a fact of life. God means for it to be so, and the Bible declares it in many places. Biblically, mystery has to do with the "hidden things" of God (prophetically in Job 28:11; Ps. 78:2; Isa. 48:6; Dan. 2:22), which He reveals to His people as and when He chooses. The apostle Paul brings it up at least sixteen times in his letters to the very first Christians—to the churches in Rome, Corinth, Ephesus, Colossae, and Thessalonica—and personally to Timothy. The unveiling of God's mystery is found in Christ and the church, including our (and your) part and participation as Christians.

Still, mystery remains, and we accept it and rejoice in it because it has mostly to do with the fact that God is God, and we are not. The unveiling of it shows us who He is, what He is like, and what He has done.

But mystery does not necessarily remain *mysterious* for us as believers. We must remember what we just said: these are hidden things that *He reveals*. He does not leave us in the dark. Part of the ministry of the Holy Spirit is the shedding of light on what had been mysterious but is now ready to help us in our progress toward knowing God and experiencing all He desires to share with us. God, in ways we will discuss, makes plain what He desires for us and from us. He promises glory (Rom. 8:18–19), and His Word, the Bible, is the road map to glory for us.

Attention and Understanding Required

This road map has been given to us without reservation, available to all of us to read and ponder. But if it is to guide us, it requires both our attention and our understanding. Attention is our responsibility; the understanding comes from God through the Holy Spirit, when we ask. The Spirit is available, day and night, to give understanding. How we give attention and how we submit ourselves to allow the Spirit to bring understanding are the major emphases of this book.

The Bible Is about God

The Bible has sometimes been called "God's autobiography." In it, He is revealing Himself to men and women at many times and in diverse places and ways. We must ask, "Why is He revealing Himself?" The only answer that makes sense is that He wants us to know Him.

Again: Why? Does *He* need anything from *us?*

Nothing that we can see—except that He *wants a relationship with us.* That's it. He wants us to know Him so we can have a relationship with Him. The massive effort He has given to this task says that it is very important to Him. He made us in His image, and He is in the process of bringing us back into fellowship with Him in spite of our sin. He has made us for this relationship, and in Christ He has reignited the spark that was lost to sin.

The Relationship Is Reality

In human life, relationship is the way of knowing and enjoying one another. Relationship between God and us is exactly the same. The difference is that the relationship with God is eternal. It is a present possession, but it does not end when this life is over. In that sense the relationship is the essence of reality. It is not subject to the limits of time and space. Those are temporal, created things. Our relationship with God—achieved through the atoning work of Christ—is eternal.

There Is a Way

There is a way to this relationship, made plain in the Word of God. We picture that way as a journey—a journey to higher ground. That is what this book is about. We have sought to simplify it for the purpose of introduction and encouragement; we leave comprehensive analysis to others. We present it, as clearly and simply as we can, in three parts. Each part has its role to play in our journey to higher ground, its own body of truth to declare:

1. *Relationship requires attention.* We must determine to spend time alone with God. He invites us into His presence, and it is there that we get to know Him. It begins in the daily quiet time—a necessary step.

2. *Relationship is built upon knowledge and understanding.* As we get to know Him, we also get to know about Him—what He is like, what He has done for us, what He expects of us, and how He has provided this way for us. There are facts of the Christian life, both privileges and requirements, that need our attention. In this book we seek to help the reader with those things.

3. *This relationship is founded, fostered, and nourished through prayer.* We seek to bring a deeper understanding of prayer through the clear teaching of Jesus, then offer what we have discovered to be the greatest single factor in the deepening of the prayer life—incorporating the Word of God in our prayers! It is kingdom praying, which can only be done on higher ground.

Our Aim and Our Method

As with everything in the Christian life, our relationship with the Father is centered upon the life and work of the Son, Jesus Christ. In this book, we give much attention to Him, as the living Word, and to the written Word in which we see Him as God's full and final revelation of Himself to us (Heb. 1:1–3). We also devote space to our own responses to Him—faith, obedience, and commitment.

We have done all of this praying that it will give readers a realization that prayer is God's chosen instrument for lifting us to higher levels in this growing and expanding relationship.

On to the Higher Ground

We will build on the foundation of the example and our Lord's teaching in the what, why, and how of prayer—and then seek to accomplish what the writer to the Hebrews must have had in mind when he wrote, "Therefore let us leave the elementary doctrine of Christ and go on to maturity" (Heb. 6:1a ESV).

God permitting, we will do just that—go on to maturity in our relationship with the Father—step by step, on the path of prayer. By His grace, we will find higher ground, gaining deeper truth as we go. We will make progress together.

Part 1

Preparation
for the Journey

CHAPTER 1

Starting Point

When we first come to saving faith in Christ, we're at what must be called *ground level*—learning the basics of what our Christian life is meant to be, establishing the foundation of that life. We have received Christ and become children of God (John 1:12); we have confessed Him as Savior and Lord (Rom. 10:9); and we are now new creations in Christ (2 Cor. 5:17), indwelt by the Spirit (Acts 2:38–39).

At this place of beginning, many of us are not even aware that there is higher ground waiting for us. The focus of this book—drawing ever closer to God through prayer and living in the spiritual intimacy of a personal relationship with Him—may sound like something for spiritual giants. But it is for all of us. When God knows we're ready, He will begin to stir our hearts and open our eyes to see that there is more to discover, giving us a growing sense of excitement and anticipation that we—even as raw beginners—might actually find our way onto the path to higher ground.

Wherever you are in your walk with God, just remember that we all begin at ground level. But there is more ahead.

Moving Higher Is a Choice

When we begin to realize that there is higher ground for us to seek, we have a choice to make: will we opt to stay at ground level, or will we reach for higher ground?

Some will obey their better judgment and be eager to find higher ground. Others may disregard God's prompting, realizing that higher ground for them may be "out there somewhere," but declining to move in that direction. They have their reasons: *Where would I find the time? Or the energy? What challenges might I have to face?*

After all, the Christian life at ground level has a way of becoming comfortable for many; it's manageable, and it fits well into their lifestyles. So they sit tight, or even drift aimlessly, never coming higher, failing to connect with the Lord personally, missing His best for them. They begin well, but they continue on, just moving laterally at ground level.

The problem with drifting is that it is quite easy to do, and it rarely has the look of disobedience. It is most often a path that seems like following God but will not draw us nearer to Him—and will not allow us to accomplish His greatest purposes for our lives.

I, Jim, can testify to that. Early in my life, I spent eleven years as a midlevel executive in a fine Christian denominational agency. I was respected and respectable, but the job became a shelter for drifting. Although I appeared to be serving God purposefully, I was, in fact, avoiding the primary call to ministry that I had received from God as a teenager. I was doing a good job and I was well treated, but I realized I wanted something else. Eventually, I left and started my own business, yet I continued to drift for twenty-five years more.

Finally, God caused me to see myself—and to see Him—in the clear light of day. At the age of fifty-six, God spoke clearly to me and gave me another chance. You've heard it said that He is the God of the second chance, and Kaye and I affirm the truth of it. God reached for Kaye at the same time He spoke to me. She was forty-six, and even though she'd been in church regularly throughout most of her life, she realized she had never surrendered her life to Christ. So she did that, and together the two of us finally began to *grow* in Christ.

Avoid the Drift

Our advice is: Don't drift. Take God at His word, early. But if you have drifted, don't despair. Turn to Him now, and allow Him to make of your life what only He can. For years Kaye and I drifted aimlessly, simply going through the motions, but God in His grace has redeemed those years.

You may know someone like us or—to some degree—you might share our experience. Let us encourage you: our lives prove that it is never too late to begin your journey. It's never too late to reach for higher ground!

Where Are You in Your Journey?

As we begin to take our look at higher ground, it will be helpful for you to discover where you are now in your spiritual life. Are you making progress in your journey toward a sensitive and fulfilled personal relationship with God? Or are your prayer life, Bible study, and time with God the same today as they were a year ago? two years? five?

Ask yourself some questions: Have you grown in your spiritual life? In what way? Where do you see progress? Where do you feel a need?

If you see little or no progress, this is where you must begin—or begin *again*—as we did. Ask God to help you develop the foundation that you realize you have missed. He can and will redeem the years. If, on the other hand, you are already on your way and have reached one or more levels of higher ground, realize that God is now preparing you to come higher than you've ever been. In either case, fasten your seat belt—you're in for a ride!

Anticipating the Journey— and the Destination

The journey to higher ground begins wherever each of us finds ourselves. Even as spiritual infants, growth is our desire. And as we grow, we develop an appetite for growth that cannot be satisfied if we stand still.

Granted, at first we may know only enough to say yes when we get that nudge within us urging us to seek more than we have experienced. We know that there is a journey ahead, though we have no idea what it will be like. We can only sense that God has something higher for us to seek.

As we travel, we begin to realize that the "something" toward which we are moving is God Himself. He wants us to know Him, to have fellowship with Him. Fellowship—that person-to-person relationship with our Creator—is what we were made for, and we cannot be content without it.

Our journey will take us in orderly steps to the mounds, then to the hills, and ultimately to the mountain. It is the journey of the Christian life as God means for us to live it. That nudge in our hearts has come from the Spirit of Christ, given to us by Jesus Himself to be our companion and guide on the journey.

It is God who stirs our hearts toward higher ground, and if we choose to move in that direction, He will make sure we get there. The road won't be the same for everyone because we will make different choices along the way; you may move toward one hill, while we start for another one. But we must all begin at the same place—in the daily quiet time where the relationship is discovered and from which it is nurtured. Our daily quiet time is the lifeline for our journey, and we can never be disconnected from it. If that should ever happen, we'll know it, and we'll have to come back and begin again.

Begin in the Quiet Time

Because prayer is what moves us forward, we must consider what prayer is, how we do it, and what it consists of—all fundamental truths upon which we can begin to grow and build our relationship with God. The proper starting point for discovering these truths is our daily quiet time.

While teaching His disciples, Jesus Himself emphasized this need for time alone with God—what we call quiet time—as necessary for the prayer life of a disciple.

To better understand what we're saying, please walk with us (and with Him) through movements in the spiritual development of the disciples that we find in the Gospels.

Fundamental to our understanding is an incident recorded in Luke 11:1: "[Jesus] was praying in a certain place, and when He finished, one of His disciples said to Him, 'Lord, teach us to pray.'"

Does this say to you what it said to us some years ago when we read it and began to understand its deeper truth? It is this: Prayer can be taught; and if it can be taught, it must be learned.

We aren't born (or even *born again*) knowing how to pray, at least not knowing how to do it *as God desires us to do it.*

Why did the disciples ask that question? We think it was because as they lived and walked with Jesus day by day, they saw that His life was a life of prayer. He was always at it. And when He prayed, significant things happened. They saw that His relationship with His heavenly Father was such that His prayers brought results. So they asked, and He taught them. In the matter of prayer, Jesus will be *our* teacher too.

Daily Time with God

Jesus taught that we must have *a daily time with God:* "When you pray, go into your private room, shut your door, and pray to your Father who is in secret. And your Father who sees in secret will reward you" (Matt. 6:6).

Jesus' mandate for a quiet time comes very early in His guidance for His disciples. In the Old Testament there are many examples of prayers, but no specific instructions or guidelines for prayer. In His Sermon on the Mount, Jesus began teaching His disciples how to pray. It was the beginning of His ministry; they were His first followers, so He was obviously giving them first steps, the basic necessities for building a solid foundation for a life of prayer.

We are His disciples too. As we look to His teaching of those men, we realize that we too must follow these essential steps of prayer before we can venture on to higher ground. We must first start by applying this basic fundamental truth about prayer to our lives as Jesus taught it, investing ourselves in a daily pattern of personal prayer that will make a consistent relationship with God the heart and reality of our Christian walk.

The Truth of Jesus' Teaching

Jesus' "shut the door" instruction is not about finding a room with a door, but finding time to be alone with God, away from all distractions, where we can close out the noise of daily life and routine. It's anywhere that we can give God our full attention and have the solitude we've just spoken of. It's important for us to note that Jesus didn't say, "Spend time with God when you're not too tired or busy or on vacation." He didn't qualify these statements at all.

Some might observe that Jesus didn't actually say we must go into our private room every day. That's true; in this verse He didn't. But in the example of how to pray once we "shut the door," He clearly states we should ask for our "daily bread" (Matt. 6:11). There is no doubt that He intends this to mean every day. It's our responsibility to find a way and make it a personal priority. When we do, the second part of this verse gives a remarkable promise: "But when you pray, go into your private room, shut your door, and pray to your Father who is in secret. And your Father who sees in secret will reward you" (Matt. 6:6).

Jesus promises us that we will be rewarded when we make the effort to find time to be alone with God every day. He doesn't specify what the reward is, but the first thing that comes to our minds is that the Father's reward is Himself—the personal relationship and spiritual intimacy with Him that is meant to be the heart of our prayer lives.

Knowing God Personally

Have we let that truth sink in? That this is Almighty God who is willing for us to know Him in a personal way? To enjoy spiritual intimacy with Him? "This is what the LORD says: The wise must not boast in his wisdom; the mighty must not boast in his might; the rich must not boast in his riches. But the one who boasts should boast in this, that he understands and *knows* Me" (Jer. 9:23–24, emphasis added).

The word *knows* in the above verse is *yada* in Hebrew. It means "to know through experience (rather than simply having factual knowledge), a firsthand knowing." There is a similar word in New Testament Greek that is used to translate *know* in John 17:3: "This is eternal life: that they may *know* You, the only true God, and the One You have sent—Jesus Christ" (emphasis added). The word *know* used here is *ginosko.* Like the Hebrew *yada,* it means to know through experience, and it carries the sense of a continuing personal relationship that is becoming progressively more deeply intimate.

This idea of personal relationship and intimacy is further developed by the apostle John as he speaks of the fellowship he and the other disciples enjoyed with the Father and His Son: "What we have seen and heard we also declare to you, so that you may have *fellowship* along with us; and indeed our *fellowship* is with the Father and with His Son Jesus Christ" (1 John 1:3, emphasis added). Here the word emphasized is *fellowship,* translated from the New Testament Greek *koinonia,* which has the meaning of intimacy, in this case spiritual intimacy.

It is amazing that such a relationship is even available; and of course, it has been made possible by Christ, the Way (John 14:6), our way to the Father. Perhaps even more remarkable is the understanding that it is God who is drawing us to Himself and enabling us to come (John 6:44a, 65b NIV). Jesus said we can do nothing on our own (John 15:5b), and that certainly includes nothing of spiritual growth or maturity, or reaching higher ground. He reaches for us; He pulls us closer. He initiates the desire in our hearts, opens the door of understanding, and makes it happen—if we're willing.

What Is Spiritual Intimacy with God Like?

For each person, spiritual intimacy with God is different and unique, just as personal relationships with family and friends are unique based on personalities and many other factors. But in general, the intimacy of the personal relationship with God is grounded in our growing ability to discern how He speaks to us. Jesus says His sheep will know His voice (John 10:4); they'll recognize and be familiar with it. He also says His sheep will know (*ginosko*) Him, have a progressively intimate personal relationship with Him. Sheep must learn their shepherd's voice, and they do so by being with him and knowing him ever more closely. That's also how it's meant to be with us. As we know God and become closer and closer to Him personally—understanding through the Word who He is revealed to be, how He works in the world, and what He expects of us—we learn to discern His voice.

Where does this happen? It happens in our daily quiet time with God. That is why the quiet time is not an option. It's the means by which we discover and maintain the relationship.

Knowing What to Do

We must always begin at the quiet time, and if we ever find ourselves drifting away—losing the sense of intimacy and fellowship with God—it's important to come back to this starting point and begin again. Drifting away sometimes happens, even with those who have a well-established relationship with God and a mature prayer life, especially if life circumstances or daily schedules change. If that happens, the remedy is simple: turn back to the basic principles of prayer that Jesus said we must follow. Whatever else goes on in our Christian walk, the most essential thing is to maintain this strong foundation. It's where our relationship with God is nurtured; it's where the Bible takes on personal application for us; and it's where we are prepared for even higher ground in prayer.

Starting now, and throughout the rest of this book, we'll provide opportunities for you to pray and reflect upon what you've read. Part 2, for example, is devoted to the principles of prayer that Jesus taught, and part 3 focuses on the power of praying God's Word—incorporating Scripture in our prayers. At various points we also have provided questions to guide you in reviewing each principle or example, considering how you're now applying it to your prayer life (or how you plan to), and what your prayers over the past few days or weeks actually reveal. We hope this will be both an encouragement and a challenge to you as you realize you've already been doing many, perhaps all, of the things Jesus taught. If so, it will be a clear indication that you are ready to expand your prayer life, to move toward the next level of higher ground and deeper truth. The challenge will be to take whatever next step God reveals that He wants you to take.

REFLECTION

Date_____

To Consider: How consistent are you in having your daily time with God?

On average, how many days a week do you have your quiet time?

_____

How long do you typically spend? _____

What percentage of that time is spent in prayer?_____

In reading the Bible?_____

In reading a devotional book?_____

Have you determined a time of day that works best for you
most of the time? _____

If yes, when is it? _____

As a rule, how often are you able to meet that desired schedule?
_____

If no, what is your biggest hindrance to having a set time? ____
_____

What is the most important thing to you about your daily time
with God? _____

_____

_____

_____

_____

_____

What is your greatest need regarding this daily time? _____

_____

_____

_____

_____

_____

_____

Pause now, and pray about it. Make notes as you ask God specifically for what you need.

_____

_____

_____

_____

_____

_____

_____

You may want to add this prayer to your own.

> *Father, I look to You as One*
> *who has created me in Your image,*
> *making it possible for me to know and love You in a personal way.*
> *May the Spirit of wisdom and revelation reveal You to me;*
> *May my roots go deep down into the nourishment of Your love.*
> *Grant this request in such a way that as Your child*
> *I will enjoy a daily quiet time with You*
> *that will become increasingly*
> *more consistent and fruitful than it has ever been.*
> *Thank You, Lord, for being my Teacher,*
> *for Your unfailing kindness toward me,*
> *for Your patience and Your presence,*
> *for being there when I need You.*
> *In Jesus' name I pray, amen.*

CHAPTER 2

Jesus Christ: The Way, the Truth, and the Life

This higher-ground relationship with God that we speak of—how is it possible? We can be overwhelmed by the thought of knowing God, of hearing His voice (will it be *audible?*). We are so busy that it is difficult to arrange for even *one* quiet time—and we should have it *daily?*

Objections arise. It's easy to simply give up at this point, if we put the quiet time in the same category with mowing the lawn, grocery shopping, or any of the things that line up as duties waiting for our attention.

However, the quiet time is not a chore to be scheduled. It is a daily meeting with One who loves us and desires to reveal that love by inviting us into His presence. There we can have our spiritual eyes opened and our ears unstopped to discover deep, eternal truth that will sustain us in life's most difficult times. Is that worth getting up a little early for?

The *yada* and *ginosko* kind of intimacy with God is a treasure to be found, not a goal to strive for. It is not success, but "joy unspeakable," as the Bible says (1 Pet. 1:8 KJV).

And the wonderful thing is that the door has been opened, the invitation issued, and the table set for us. It is Jesus Himself who has made our arrangements. He who has all power, all authority in heaven and earth (Matt. 28:18), is reaching out to take our hand—every morning—to lead us to the Father. There we find that priceless relationship ready to be cultivated and nourished.

It is by His mighty power that our time can be protected, distractions eliminated, truth revealed, and confidence built—all in the space of just a bit of time, our only sacrifice. His sacrifice was much greater.

Just realize that as your life of intimacy with the Father and the Son is nurtured in your quiet time each day, you are moving in measured steps toward the higher ground of that relationship for which you were made. God is waiting, Christ is leading, and the Holy Spirit is strengthening you.

It is important now to give full attention to the One upon whose life and work the relationship is built, and through whom it leads us to the higher ground.

Your Guide and Companion on the Way

Here's a biblical question for you: What was Jesus doing during those three years when twelve chosen men walked with Him, listened to His teaching, observed His miracles, and were radically changed in the process?

Answer: He was leading them to *higher ground.*

Step by step, He took them—trusting Him, but needing to be taught—and revealed to them just who He was and what He had come to do. Then, after He had done what He came to do—in His death on the cross and His resurrection and ascension—He revealed to them the eternal glory that is His and would be theirs—and ours. What they learned, and only slowly comprehended, was *deeper truth*—about His person, His identity, His redemptive purpose, His unique place as both God and man.

Are we being presumptuous to see ourselves, beyond the limits of time and space, as virtual mirror images of those twelve?

It's really not presumptuous at all. You are in the same relationship with Jesus as were those disciples. He chose you. As you observe how Jesus led them, what He taught, and how He lived His life before them, you see clearly that their movement to higher spiritual ground was not a miraculous, instantaneous transformation, but a *process.* There were steps to take.

A Sequence of Steps

The deeper truth would not—indeed, could not—come all at once. Jesus led His disciples just as He leads you—gently but relentlessly—to become the instruments that the Father could use in His kingdom-building enterprise. They had to be spoon-fed at first, but in the end they became bold, fearless examples of what God desires to accomplish in all of us.

That process—Jesus leading and His disciples following—is the same for you today. You are His disciple, just as they were. There is higher ground for you. The rocky but well-marked path that leads you upward—as it led them—is a sequence of steps, not a single leap. Walking daily with the Master, always toward the higher ground, they were also made ready for deeper truth, as you will be. The key is in the daily walk and the willingness to listen—and to learn.

The higher ground is waiting to receive you if you desire to find it—to experience more of God's presence and power, thereby achieving the inner peace and outer strength that come from an intimate and growing relationship with Him.

A Prevailing Personal Problem

Many Christians today may find it difficult to commit discipline, time, and energy to even a brief daily quiet time because they have bought into the worldly concept that life is divided into two areas: the *sacred* and the *secular.* To them the *sacred* means going to church, engaging in Bible study, finding some time to pray, and attending an occasional spiritual retreat or conference. The *secular,* on the other hand, is everything else: family, career, hobbies, vacations, etc.

In a life committed to God, there is no separation between the sacred and the secular. The life of the Christian is to be consistent and focused, honoring to God in the home, at school, in the workplace—everywhere. All is sacred in the eye of God and in the eye of His child. Those things seen as secular have little or no connection with the inner life, the relationship with God. For many people with secular mind-sets—some Christians included—God would only get in the way.

Strangely, many of these folks would really like to find the higher ground. They are occasionally motivated—after hearing a stirring sermon or reading something by C. S. Lewis, J. I. Packer, or Henry Blackaby—to resolve to seek what is higher.

Therein lies their main problem. They are convinced that the higher ground can be reached by resolve. It cannot. It can only be reached by relationship—a relationship built upon the life that is in Christ, which He shares with all who will receive it.

We mention these things as a caution for all of us. We should be on our guard against the compartmentalizing of life.

It is an attitude prevalent in the body of Christ as well as in the world.

The Heart of the Matter

Jesus declares, "I am the way, the truth, and the life. No one comes to the Father except through Me" (John 14:6). He is not speaking a poetic platitude to make us think in other-worldly ways. He is taking His position at the center of life for the believer. He says that it all focuses on Him, hinges on Him, depends upon Him. Whatever we have to gain in this world and in the world to come will be found in Him, and nowhere else.

He is it.

Until we have settled this matter in our hearts and minds—that everything God has to give us is in Christ and in Him alone—we are not prepared to seek higher ground or to receive deeper truth.

Consider it a matter of perspective and of viewpoint. If you've watched your own children grow, you have been amazed at how they change at various seasons of their lives. From loving, dependent, obedient (hopefully) pre-teens, they may turn into self-centered, rebellious seekers of peer acceptance in their teenage years—often with dire consequences. If this is not true of your kids, praise God! But read the newspaper or watch TV for the story of many of today's youth. It can be frightening.

Watching those changes in our children can be painful—but also very symbolic of human life itself. We all constantly undergo change. And without intervention, that change will always be on a downward course. But "Jesus Christ is the same yesterday, today, and forever" (Heb. 13:8). How important is stability in your life? You can't keep your children from growing older, but in Christ they—and you—can walk with firm steps through the downward drag of the culture that surrounds us all.

His Steady Hand, Leading

That is the satisfaction that is in Christ. It is stability, reliability, steadfastness in the face of unwelcome and unwholesome influences that the world brings. He Himself brings change, but it is always change for the better. The change is to what is higher—higher ground for your life, higher aims for your family, higher hopes for those you care for.

The glory of knowing Christ changes our perspectives and our viewpoints. Bit by bit, we become aware that He is truly "all in all" for us. Our love for Him and our desire to follow Him do not replace our love for family and friends or our desire for good things from this life. What changes is our awareness of what things are truly worth desiring, and then we see Him as supreme in that view of life. Children, family, work, leisure— all take on new delight as we delight first in Him, seeing Him as the Way, the Truth, and the Life *in all those things.*

The Deeper Truth

John 14:6 *is* the deeper truth. Our life, our hope, our eternal good—all are found in Christ. It is true of this present life as well as the next. In sharing Himself with us, Christ is leading us to seek to be with Him, where He is.

The higher ground is where He is. In His humanity He walked as we walk, leading His disciples as He desires to lead us. Higher ground: He is there, ready to encourage and to lift us— always to bring us nearer to Him than we are at the moment.

But can we actually be where He is?

When He was about to depart this earth, to return to the Father, He said it this way: "And remember, *I am with you* always" (Matt. 28:20, emphasis added). He made this promise to a bunch of men who were about to embark on a mission that would call for maximum courage and total commitment. It would call for more than they possessed, but His promise was "I am with you." Though out of sight, He would be present to supply whatever would be needed. They would be able to do what He had spent three years preparing them to do. They would be His witnesses to the world. They would reach higher ground because He would be with them.

And He will be with you as you accept and acknowledge Him as your Way, your Truth, your Life.

Christ Is the Way

What does this mean to us? In the first place, it means that without Him our relationship with the Father would be impossible. He is the "torn curtain" of Hebrews 10:20, through which we enter the presence of the Father. His life was poured out on the cross to give us this privilege. It is why He died. We who were born enemies of God have been reconciled to Him by the blood of His Son, Jesus Christ.

So when we present Jesus as the Way, we are saying, "Don't take another step in your journey to higher ground if you expect to reach it by any other path—any other way." There is no other way. The higher ground of greater fellowship with God, of our own spiritual growth and usefulness, can be found only in Jesus Christ, the Way.

Here, too, we experience the deeper truth.

Not by Works

Not really deep, we say? We've always known this. It is a fundamental fact of our faith. But is it a fact in practice as well as in belief? Do we declare it to be true, and then seek higher ground by a life of good works? Are we spending and being spent in doing good deeds, things that others recommend?

Good works are a part of the Christian life, of course. But the greater work of Jesus Christ on the cross has set us free from any thought that our good works will play a part in God's acceptance of us. We are accepted because of the atoning sacrifice of Christ on the cross. We are righteous in the Father's sight because we are in Christ, and there is no other standard applied. Paul says in his letter to the Ephesians, "For by grace you are saved through faith, and this is not from yourselves; it is God's gift—not from works, so that no one can boast. For we are His creation—created in Christ Jesus for good works, which God prepared ahead of time so that we should walk in them" (Eph. 2:8–10).

The Way of the Cross

Many people find it difficult to understand the true nature of the sacrificial death of Jesus on the cross. Why was it necessary? What did God have in mind, and why couldn't He have brought us to Himself for eternity by some other method?

One reason we may find it difficult is that we see it as *punishment*—the Father punishing His own Son because of something the rest of us have done. (Jesus never sinned, so why punish Him?) Punishing one person for another person's sin seems unfair, to say the least, from any perspective of human logic and reasoning.

These are reasonable questions, certainly, if we think of Christ on the cross as punishment in the same way we think of a prison sentence—or even the death penalty—as punishment for breaking the law.

But look at it another way. Consider it rather as payment of a debt. It makes sense for a debt to be paid by a person who has resources, on behalf of someone who has none. That is a common occurrence in our world—one person stepping in to pay a debt on behalf of another who is unable to pay it on his own.

When man sinned (in the person of Adam, the first man), he began a process within which each man (and woman) since also has sinned. Sin is an act of rebellion against a God who gave us life and requires something of us in return. What He requires is what we cannot do—live the kind of life He intended for Adam, perfect and complete. We owe Him that.

But sin is in our nature; we inherited that as a result of Adam's fall. It has been well said that we are not sinners because we sin; we sin because we are sinners. We are born sinners, and God cannot look upon sin. He could only collect the debt by paying the debt Himself. We have no resources within ourselves to make the payment.

But God Himself, as God, is perfect and could not be the sacrifice required for the payment. He had to become a man; man had to pay the debt. And there was only one man who had no sin, who could thus meet the requirement. He was God who became Man, Jesus Christ. He paid the debt on the cross.

Our Debt Is Paid

The old hymn says it: *Jesus paid it all.* The debt has been paid in full. At the cross, He not only opened the way, He became the Way. As Peter declared boldly in the earliest days after the cross: "Salvation is found in no one else, for there is no other name under heaven given to men by which we must be saved" (Acts 4:12 NIV). This is the glorious truth we declare along with Peter, rejoicing with the redeemed of all the ages. Jesus, alive in His resurrected glory, is our Way into the presence, the joy, the glory of the Father. He is the Way along the way—the Way for us on our way to higher ground. There is no other way, but praise God we have the Way!

Christ Is the Truth

When Jesus declared Himself to be "the truth" in John 14:6, He gave further testimony of the reality of who He is. He had said to His disciples: "I am going away to prepare a place for you. If I go away and prepare a place for you, I will come back and receive you to Myself, so that where I am you may be also. You know the way where I am going" (John 14:2–4). But the disciples thought otherwise. In fact, it was Thomas who voiced the group's question: they had *no idea* where He was going, so how could they know the way?

Jesus responded with something even further beyond their comprehension—that while He was their Way, He was *more* than the Way. He was, in fact "the way, the truth, and the life" (John 14:6).

Into New Territory

It is evident at this point—on the very last night of His earthly life—that Jesus was taking those eleven remaining men into new territory in their thinking. Here they were, still uncertain, still lacking the awareness that would equip them for the work He would leave them to do as He went to the cross and then back to the Father's side.

In the very same way, and with the same words, our Master takes us into new territory as we climb with Him onto new plateaus of spiritual knowledge and experience.

A necessary element of the journey is His unveiling of deeper truth—the kind of truth that we must have if we are to be prepared, as the disciples would be, for life in a hostile world and then for life in a glorious eternity. Preparation for both is necessary.

The Truth Is about . . . Himself

We must continue to emphasize that Jesus takes the disciples—including us—to a deeper understanding of Himself—of who He is, and then of who we are as we find our life in Him.

So on our pilgrimage with Him, looking always to higher ground, He brings us to the deeper truth that gives us confidence to keep going. If not for our hope—indeed our certainty—in Him, how can we make it through life's minefields? The answer is, we can't. Yet many try, not deliberately but by default and neglect. When we fail to live in the relationship that Christ makes possible and that God desires—when we fail to invest ourselves in the daily time through which we get to know Him, to discern where He is leading—we may be in the minefields all the time.

Jesus, the very Son of God, knows what we need to know. And the first thing we need to know is that He is God in the flesh, and that He has given us the same promise He spoke that night in the Upper Room as He was saying farewell to the fearful men He would leave behind: "I will not leave you as orphans; I am coming to you. In a little while the world will see Me no longer, but you will see Me. Because I live, you will live too" (John 14:18–19).

His promise is sure. He has not left us alone, unattended on life's journey. The world can no longer see Him, but we, His own, have Him with us at all times. That is because His life is in us, through the presence of the Holy Spirit, who is our guide for life. Yet it's up to us to maintain our vital connection with Him—the thing that gives us sensitivity to His presence. And it doesn't just happen; it must be cultivated.

A vital part of the deeper truth that Jesus has to give is that we are not alone. He lives within us. We'll say much more about this in the next section as we discover what Jesus means when He says He is "the *Life*." That is, He is our life on this higher ground we seek. That fact is deeper truth. It is the mystery hidden from the ages: Christ still and forever alive in you—"the hope of glory" (Col. 1:27).

What Does This Mean for You Today?

The deeper truth is what the world cannot see. It is life. When we serve the world and accept its ways of thinking and acting, we are blind to the deeper truth of the Christ-life that brings joy and real success and lasts for eternity.

But now, friend, you are not blind. You have set your course for the higher ground, and—with Christ as your companion and guide—you're already finding it.

Christ Is the Life

In Galatians 2:20, the apostle Paul wrote, "I am crucified with Christ: nevertheless I live; yet not I, but Christ liveth in me: and the life which I now live in the flesh I live by the faith of the Son of God, who loved me, and gave himself for me" (Gal. 2:20 KJV). For this verse, we go to the King James Version, which alone gives the reading found in the midsection of the verse: "I live by *the faith of* the Son of God" (emphasis added). Here is something very significant: *Christ lives in me.* The life in Christ and the life in me are *the same life!* But then, it is a life that hinges on *His* faith, not mine. Our faith is in Him, and we're much better off counting on—and living by—His faith, His life, granted to us and living in us, than anything that might issue from our own inner self.

Perhaps the point is not necessary to make; other versions of the Bible are not wrong in saying that we live by faith *in* the Son of God. Of course we do. But consider the strength of Paul's statement as we present it.

Jesus has given you His life, not just a different (and better) kind of human life. Realize this: because He has planted His Spirit within you, He has given you His life, and He is living out His life on earth, today, in you. And in us. And in all who make up His earthly body, the church. This is His promise of abundant life as He says plainly: "I have come that they may have life and have it in abundance" (John 10:10). This, we believe, is the heart of what He meant when He spoke the words recorded in John 14:6, "I am the way, the truth, and the life." In fact, let's look at John's earlier words in the very opening of his Gospel account: "In the beginning was the Word, and the Word was with God, and the Word was God. . . . In him was life, and the life was the light of men" (John 1:1, 4 ESV). The Lord Jesus, Son of God, is portrayed by John as "the Word." What is a word? It is an expression of a concept, an idea, a truth. It is through words that we express ourselves. And it is through the Word, Jesus Christ, that God the Father has expressed Himself to us and to all who will listen.

The Word in the Flesh

So the Word became flesh. In Him was life. He became man in order to share His own life with men. The life He took upon Himself "in the likeness of sinful flesh" (Rom. 8:4) He gave in sacrifice on the cross, to be our sin-bearer. But He brought another, more enduring kind of life, an endless life that He gives through His Holy Spirit, living within every believer.

He spoke much about this enduring, eternal kind of life. For example, in John 6:32–33 He spoke of Himself as life-giving Bread: "Moses didn't give you the bread from heaven, but My Father gives you the real bread from heaven. For the bread of God is the One who comes down from heaven and gives life to the world."

Jesus presented Himself graphically in so many ways—not only as the bread of life but also as the living water and the Good Shepherd, who gives eternal life to the sheep: "My sheep hear My voice, I know them, and they follow Me. I give them eternal life, and they will never perish—ever! No one will snatch them out of My hand" (John 10:27–28).

Further, He shows Himself not only as the giver of life, but as life itself. Remember His words to His friend Martha when she expressed her grief over the death of her brother Lazarus: "Jesus said to her, 'I am the resurrection and the life. The one who believes in Me, even if he dies, will live. Everyone who lives and believes in Me will never die—ever. Do you believe this?'" (John 11:25–26). Martha was perceptive enough, and knew Him well enough, to answer for all of us: "'Yes, Lord,' she told Him, 'I believe You are the Messiah, the Son of God, who was to come into the world'" (John 11:27).

The Vine and the Branches

Beyond all other examples is this: "I am the vine; you are the branches. The one who remains in Me and I in him produces much fruit, because you can do nothing without Me" (John 15:5). What a picture this is! Think of a luxurious vine on which branches are growing, branches bearing grapes in profusion. What Jesus says is that He, the Vine, is the source of life—both for the branches and for the grapes they bear. Nourishment comes from the vine and into the branches so they can be alive and fruitful. Branches live because the vine is alive. As long as the vine is alive, the branches can be alive. The vine *is* the life of the branches.

In the same way, Jesus says, He is our life. While we are attached to Him—in constant contact and open to the flow of His life into us—we have life. Abundant life.

This is the personal relationship of spiritual intimacy that our Lord wants us to have! He has given us spirit, soul, and body so that our spirit can be ignited by His Spirit and our body energized for a life that reflects His presence. That's what the abundant life should look like. But it doesn't (can't?) happen in the normal, routine busyness of life as we tend to live it. Abundant life begins in the daily quiet time, and it continues as our prayer life becomes the mainspring that regulates all of our life.

It just isn't possible for fruit to be borne from branches that are not open to the flow of the vine's pulsing life. Without nurturing the relationship, we find ourselves struggling to produce fruit in our own strength—and it doesn't work!

So How Can This Be True of Your Life?

It *is* true, by God's grace, when you become a believer in Christ. A believer, that is, who is not just a church member, or the child of Christian parents, or one who has prayed a certain kind of prayer. A Christian believer is one in whom the life of Jesus is a present and eternal reality—one who has made the unbreakable commitment to receive Christ's life and to live for Him, thus sharing in His life now and forever. As the book of Hebrews states it: "For if we are faithful to the end, trusting God just as firmly as when we first believed, we will share in all that belongs to Christ" (3:14 NLT).

The Great Secret

The apostle Paul speaks of this Christ-life in us as a "mystery": "the mystery hidden for ages and generations but now revealed to His saints. God wanted to make known . . . the glorious wealth of this mystery, which is Christ in you, the hope of glory" (Col. 1:26–27). Call it a mystery or a secret; what it means is something that God has revealed to those who come to Him through faith in Christ, thus receiving this Christ-life as a permanent, forever possession.

The Desire and the Enabling

This, then, is how Jesus Christ Himself is our way to the higher ground. It is a reflection of His life within us that we first desire to reach higher ground and then are enabled to make the journey. It is in His strength that we want the higher ground; then we make the commitment to seek it. As we move higher, step by step, hill by hill, it is His life that sustains us, energizes us, and fills us as we go.

This life that He gives is our very reason for the upward journey. It is in this fellowship with Him that we find meaning for our own life. It is the reason and the end of the search. It is life as God originally intended it to be.

The Rest of the Statement

Before we move on in our journey, let's look at the rest of Jesus' statement in John 14:6. He not only identifies Himself as Way, Truth, and Life, He makes clear that "No one comes to the Father except through Me" (John 14:6).

The deeper truth of John 14:6 is that *our real purpose is to come to the Father.* We use this verse in our evangelism—making the point that it is impossible to find salvation by any other means than through the shed blood of Jesus Christ on the cross. It is true, and we must never stray from it even for a moment.

Yet there is even more "deeper truth" here. It is not only our salvation that must be gained through Christ; it is the fellowship also. We were created to have fellowship with the Father; there can be no other explanation for His making us in the first place or for His infinite patience and ultimate sacrifice in drawing us back to Himself through the death and resurrection of the Son.

REFLECTION

Date_____

To Consider: Jesus' disciples didn't reach higher ground overnight. Describe your present relationship to Jesus as either the Way, the Truth, the Life, or the Vine. _____

_____

_____

_____

_____

_____

What is the best thing about that relationship right now?

_____

_____

_____

_____

_____

What is the most important thing you can anticipate happening with this relationship as you come to higher ground?

_____

_____

_____

_____

_____

What do you want to most improve in your relationship as branch to Jesus, your Vine? _____

_____

_____

_____

_____

Pause now, and pray about it. Ask God specifically for what you want to happen.

_____

_____

_____

_____

_____

_____

_____

You may want to add this prayer to your own.

Father, You are the One who sent Your Son
to be our Way, our Truth, our Life;
You are the One who grafted me into the Vine.
Help these word pictures to come alive in my heart and my mind
as I come ever closer to You
through my prayer life.
Lord Jesus, I want to bear Your fruit
for the Father's glory;
I want to enjoy the abundant life You have promised
so that I may serve You and Your kingdom purposes
more fully than I ever have.
Be my Way, my Truth, my Life—my Vine!
Sustain me on my journey to higher ground;
bless me with deeper truth as I choose to grow with You.
Father, I ask these things in Jesus' name, amen.

CHAPTER 3

Provision for the Journey

We come now to a natural bridge from the view of the person of Christ in the previous chapter to His prayer teaching as we will encounter it in part 2. Anticipating our journey of discovery, what do we need to know and do to be ready—first to hear from Him, then to walk with Him?

This journey, as we are learning, is a journey of prayer. It is prayer that takes us to the higher ground of the personal relationship with God, prayer that moves us ever closer to God. This kind of prayer requires something of us. We've begun rightly with the *foundation*—the daily quiet time—and we've found the proper *perspective* in the person of Christ:

- our Way into the relationship and Guide to the higher ground;
- the Truth of the reality of that relationship and its impact on our lives; and
- the Life, abundant life ignited by His presence for His kingdom purpose in and through us—a life that is realized through the relationship.

Now we fortify our minds as well as our hearts for the higher ground. We need to get ready!

Preparation for the Journey

If you intend to travel to Chicago today, you won't just drive to the airport and go from airline to airline, terminal to terminal, counter to counter, to determine if perhaps there might be a plane leaving sometime for Chicago. (Or maybe you will, but it's not a very good idea.)

What do you do? You make plans in advance (if for no other reason than the exorbitant cost of tickets purchased on the day of departure). Well before you get into the car to drive to the airport, you know exactly what flight you'll be on, when it is to depart and arrive, and all pertinent information. You leave nothing to chance. You have your ticket in your pocket, your bag is packed, and your mind, body, and shoes are ready for Homeland Security.

Sadly, far too many people seek to find God with far less confidence, preparation, and certainty than they exhibit on a trip to Chicago!

For a successful journey to higher ground, you'll need to be ready—and you'll need to understand what "ready" means.

Components of the Preparation

Three vital components of your preparation are faith, obedience, and commitment.

Why these three specifically? Perhaps you think your life calls for others as well (only God can show you what else you'll need), but these three must be addressed first. If you're like most of us, you're starting from a pretty basic level, so be sure you have the essentials in place.

Let's look at them.

Faith

If we expect to reach higher ground, we must believe that Jesus will help us get there. This is what faith is about—believing God (not just believing *in* God.) We must believe the basic things that we learn of God from His Word:

- He loves us supremely (He sent His only Son to die for us).
- He desires fellowship with us (That was His reason for creating us in the first place).
- He has prepared an eternal home for our life with Him (Read about this in Revelation).

These are only three basic beliefs, but an important three. God wants us to find Him! He's not hiding from us. Yet this journey of discovery requires that we believe Him and trust those things that we know about Him. What we learn about Him and how we get to know Him in the journey are deeper truths that we are seeking.

To put it simply, faith—a living, growing faith—is essential for our progress toward higher ground. The Bible puts the highest priority on faith, evident when we read from the letter to the Hebrews: "Now without faith it is impossible to please God, for the one who draws near to Him must believe that He exists and rewards those who seek Him" (11:6). It seems unlikely, doesn't it, that we could live in intimate fellowship with God while *dis*pleasing Him? Since we, in our flesh, can't live perfect lives, it is our faith that enables us to please Him—because our faith brings us under the cleansing power of the blood of Christ. It is in Christ that we are acceptable—pleasing—to God.

Obedience

Remember the final assignment Jesus gave to His disciples—also known as the Great Commission: "Jesus came and told his disciples, 'I have been given complete authority in heaven and on earth. Therefore, go and make disciples of all the nations, baptizing them in the name of the Father and the Son and the Holy Spirit. *Teach these new disciples to obey all the commands I have given you.* And be sure of this: I am with you always, even to the end of the age'" (Matt. 28:18–20 NLT, emphasis added). The risen Lord spoke lovingly but firmly to these men to whom He was giving the keys of His kingdom. He affirmed His unlimited authority, gave them their primary assignment—the making of disciples worldwide (with submission to baptism as a sign of identification with Him)—and then told them to "teach these new disciples to obey all the commands I have given you." Finally, He promised that His presence would always accompany them. Need we repeat that all of this is for us just as it was for those men?

Jesus' statement concerning obedience is as important as the affirmation of authority, the command to go and make disciples, the symbolism of the baptism, and the promise of His Holy Spirit's continuing and endless presence with us. Included is the injunction: Disciples must learn that obedience to His commands is a necessary part of the discipleship process.

Likewise, it is a necessary part of our progress on the journey to higher ground. Why? Because just as Jesus devoted Himself totally to the doing of the Father's will, He expects the same from His disciples. God's Word makes no room for disobedience. God's plans work when they are carried out His way. The disciples learned to do as Jesus said (remember the massive catch of fish after they had seen empty nets all night long). He taught them to pray, and He gave them no alternatives. How often we seem to look at Jesus' commands as suggestions! They are not. He gives very clear instructions, and our life works best when we follow them.

Commitment

To reach the higher ground—a climb that often taxes all of our powers at the same time—we must make an unbreakable commitment. The commitment is both to God and to ourselves. It says that we will not give up.

Christians frequently misconstrue what is meant by *commitment*—at least, in a biblical context. The most familiar point of reference is in Psalm 37: "Commit your way to the LORD; trust in Him, and He will act, making your righteousness shine like the dawn, your justice like the noonday" (vv. 5–6). Look carefully at this passage. It is a perfect illustration of so much that we find in God's Word. It is about submission—yielding of ourselves and the plans and actions of our lives—to Him. His will, revealed in ways of His choosing, becomes our will. Our obedience and compliance with the will and ways of God bring about a result that is for His glory and for the benefit of others.

What happens when we commit our way to the Lord, trusting in Him alone? First, He will *act*. He will not sit idly when we truly yield our way to Him. He will act—always in a movement that accomplishes His greater purposes for us and for our world. Then He will bring about a *shining*—a brightness that issues from our righteousness and our justice, both gifts from Him that we cannot manufacture for ourselves.

All of this is very good news for the determined, but sometimes hesitant, traveler. The responsibility for our ascent to higher ground is God's, not ours. Our job is to commit—firm determination backed by faith, characterized by obedience, and undergirded by prayer—and to stay the course. God is the One who lifts us from hill to hill. It is His strength in action, not our own.

Right now, affirm—for yourself and for your heavenly Father—your decision to commit your way to Him, with no thought of turning back. Take a look at your journey to higher ground, remembering that your purpose is a closer, richer, deeper relationship with God, and that it is *prayer* that moves you ever closer to Him.

Together, we look next in some depth at the process of prayer—the sequence in which the elements of true prayer take place. Then in part 2 we will study prayer as Jesus taught it and demonstrated it in His life. By His teaching and example, we will find higher ground for our own prayer lives.

REFLECTION

Date_____

To Consider: How well are you equipped?
Do you really have faith to believe that God *wants* a personal relationship with you that is closer than what you feel you're experiencing right now? _____

_____

Whether yes or no, pause right now and pray; ask God to show you His heart. You may want to jot down what you sensed from Him, what thoughts came to mind. _____

_____

_____

_____

If you were to rate yourself honestly regarding your level of obedience to what you already know about what God expects of your prayer life and your willingness to have a personal relationship with Him, 1 to 10 (10 being highest), how would you score yourself? And why? _____

_____

_____

_____

What would you like to improve? (There's always room for improvement!) Pause and pray about it right now, and ask God for something specific to help.

_____

_____

_____

_____

How committed are you to going forward to higher ground at this point? Again, rate yourself 1 to 10, and ask yourself why you feel that way. _____

_____

_____

_____

Pause and ask God to help you reach and maintain the level of commitment you desire.

_____

_____

_____

_____

_____

_____

_____

You may want to add this prayer to your own.

Father, You are the Lord,
and nothing is impossible for You!
I ask You to increase my faith for the journey;
grant me to believe that increased spiritual intimacy
with You is possible,
and to be willing to commit to the journey.
Help me to be ready to obey whatever You ask me to do;
help me to finish strong,
to throw off anything that could hinder me
and keep me off of the higher ground.
I thank You that I'm a work in progress,
and You aren't finished with me yet!
Spin me on Your potter's wheel and make of me
what You want me to be.
In Jesus' name, amen.

CHAPTER 4

The Prayer Process

In the pages ahead, we have much to say about prayer. In part 2 we'll look closely at Jesus' prayer teaching (with some "how to" help in praying through the elements of His model prayer), at His prayer promises, and at His own life as a Man of prayer.

When you reach part 3, you will find a challenging and enlightening introduction to the power of filling your prayers with Scripture. It's one way we believe this book will energize and expand your prayer life, helping you on the trek to higher ground.

Right now, in chapter 4, we begin to set the stage with a very practical view of the structural and sequential framework in which the act of praying finds expression. If you've never thought deeply about the mechanics of prayer, this chapter will provide a simple but illuminating look at prayer under the microscope.

Our Prayer and God's Attention

We have a God who neither slumbers nor sleeps (Ps. 121:4). Our prayers do not awaken Him, but they do somehow draw His attention.

That may be an improper way to express what we have to share in this chapter. Certainly there is nothing that is hidden from His sight, and He is more than able to take initiative to bring about His purposes—in individual lives, in entire nations, or in the whole earth. He has no limits.

Still, the biblical record testifies that once God has given instruction, encouragement, or warning to His people, He waits for them (us) to respond—either to obey or to ask wisdom and insight concerning the decisions we make and actions we take as a result of hearing from Him. In the Old Testament, men such as Job and Jonah learned lessons in that process. God lets us make our mistakes and pay the price—but He also hears the cry of a hungry or hurting heart and keeps His promises.

Earlier in this book, we began our quest for higher ground believing it to be essential to our desired relationship with God, and we determined that the means of establishing and cultivating that relationship is prayer. However, as we've seen, it is not casual, inconsistent, or shallow praying that moves us ever closer to God. Our lack of planning, our shifting priorities, and our self-focus must surely offend Him. He can hear, but He also can hide His face.

Our shallow and casual prayers may be sincere, and the needs may be urgent and compelling, but if our relationship is equally shallow and casual, we have little reason to expect Him to act as we wish Him to act.

Principles of Prayer on the Higher-Ground Journey

The prayer principles set before you in this book are primarily those Jesus taught His disciples from the earliest days of His ministry through His last hours with them before He went to the cross. He began, as any good teacher would (and He was the best), with fundamental truth about prayer. The life of prayer begins with necessary time alone with God (Matt. 6:6); He expects it, we need it, and He honors our obedience to do it. It is essential if we want the joy of living in spiritual intimacy with Him.

Jesus then proceeded with specific teaching on the content of our prayers (Matt. 6:9–13), our commitment to prayer and the intensity we bring to it (Luke 11:5–8; 18:1–8), and the results we can expect if our relationship with Him is as it should be—and if we are sensitive to ask according to His will.

Prayer that is honoring to our God must be intentional, purposeful, and sacrificial—in terms of time, effort, and energy that are involved when we pray consistently and whole-heartedly. As prayer is made in this way—becoming a daily priority and (dare we say it) *habit*—our personal relationship with the Father, through the Son and in the Spirit, becomes increasingly real and practical because it allows us to enter into meaningful conversation with God.

Prayer—not the saying-words-with-eyes-closed kind, but earnest and God-seeking—*is* practical. Prayer is, in fact, the most practical thing we can do as God's children. When we come to Him in submission—seeking to know Him and to live in His presence, accepting His blessings and obeying His loving instructions—we are building that cherished relationship with the God of heaven and earth.

It will help us now to consider what is happening when we pray.

The Prayer Dialogue

Prayer is a dialogue between two people who love each other.
ROSALIND RINKER[1]

The concept of prayer as dialogue is not new, but to many of us it is still unfamiliar, and we often find it difficult to incorporate into our thinking. It can be even more difficult if we fail to perceive God as both omnipotent Ruler and loving Father. Can it be possible that the Creator God—"Judge of all the earth" (Gen. 18:25)—and I, insignificant and unlovable, can engage in such dialogue?

If we can believe the Bible, that is exactly what happens when we pray.

In his excellent book *Whole Prayer,* Walter Wangerin Jr. reminds us of a deceptively simple but profound analysis noted by astute students of the Word.[2] Our praying, as God Himself works through it, is dialogue that essentially involves four steps:

1. We speak.
2. God listens.
3. God speaks.
4. We listen.

We will look at these four steps in some detail, and then add a fifth—a step beyond the prayer itself that we believe to be an equally important part of the cycle.

5. *If* God gives an assignment or command, we obey.

Granted, obedience is not always a necessary element of prayer. God's word to us does not always give an instruction. Often it is an affirmation of something about which we've been praying—or a bit of encouragement or revelation of His greater purposes in what He is doing in and around us.

Still, much of our praying remains incomplete because having heard a word of instruction or a command from God, we choose to evaluate it, weigh it, consider it, discuss it . . . anything but obey it. Yet our only reasonable response to His command is immediate obedience. Hold that thought for awhile as we look more closely at the five steps in the prayer dialogue.

Step 1: We Speak

I call to God Most High,
to God who fulfills His purpose for me.
PSALM 57:2

This step is always first. Of course, God can speak to us whenever and however He chooses, whether we speak first or not, but that does not constitute true prayer. That is His dynamic and purposeful intervention in our circumstances or our relationships in order to warn or to correct. It may come in a sermon, a conversation with a friend, or a Bible reading. It can come in whatever way God may select.

In true prayer, however, *we initiate.* God has arranged it that way. Recall this from the epistle of James: "*Draw near to God, and He will draw near to you. Cleanse your hands, sinners, and purify your hearts, double-minded people!*" (4:8, emphasis added). Truly, this is an amazing thing. God invites us to come near, which means that we can do just that. But we must take the lead. First we draw near to Him (in prayer), and then He will draw near to us (He listens, then speaks in response). Do you see how the principle of daily time alone with God is the key to this drawing near? We're the ones who must set aside the time and be disciplined to keep our appointment with God every day. We may ask for His help, and we'll find Him willing to give it—but we must commit to it and be willing to sacrifice the time and energy to make it happen.

Our drawing near may be through the prayerful and attentive reading of a passage of Scripture. How often does our spirit stir within us when we read (maybe for the hundredth time) a familiar verse or chapter. When the Holy Spirit prompts us to open ourselves to a fresh encounter with God in His Word, we often find this is the opening step in a vital dialogue with God.

The truth found in James 4:8 is familiar, and there are many other such invitations—some more familiar than others—throughout the Bible. God said to the prophet Jeremiah: "Call to Me and I will answer you and tell you great and wondrous things you do not know" (Jer. 33:3). Notice that God did not say "Jeremiah, stand still and listen to what I have to say." He did give such instructions on other occasions, when His servants were not in the relationship with Him that He desired, but not this time. In the right relationship, we are given the privilege—and the responsibility—to initiate the dialogue with Him.

Let us not take this lightly. While it gives us a mighty privilege to be the ones who start the conversation with the Creator, it also tells us that *nothing will likely happen until we do.* He is waiting. Waiting.

Once we realize we are to initiate the dialogue with God, our next question becomes: What do we say when we speak? This is where we pay careful attention to the teaching of Jesus, reflecting back on Matthew 6:9–13. He was not, we think, insisting that every element of that prayer teaching be incorporated in every prayer that we pray. But He was certainly speaking of priority. Let's recall the *order* of His points:

1. First comes *relationship:* **Our Father in heaven . . .** (We acknowledge the One to whom we are speaking; He is our Father.)
2. Then comes *worship:* **Hallowed be Your name . . .** (We acknowledge who He is, in all His worthiness of our worship.)
3. Then *surrender* or *submission:* **Your kingdom come, Your will be done . . .** (We acknowledge that He is God, King, Lord, Master, Creator, Almighty, and Everlasting One, to whom we owe everything.)

4. Then, we *ask to be supplied the necessities of life:* **Give us today our daily bread . . .** (We ask, not for what we *want* but for what we *need*.)

5. Then, we *confess* that we are sinners in need of forgiveness: **Forgive us our debts, as we forgive our debtors . . .** (We ask—that we might be forgiven in exactly the same way we have forgiven those who have wronged us.)

6. Then, we pray: **Do not lead us into temptation . . .** (We ask to be *spared the temptations* that could distract or set us off God's course for our lives.)

7. Then, we conclude: **. . . but deliver us from the evil one.** (We ask to be *protected* from the power and influence of Satan and his demons.)

It is when we have understood and incorporated these elements into our praying that we identify with the Lord Jesus Himself in our prayer life. We will discuss this in greater depth in chapter 6.

Step 2: God Listens

Know that the LORD has set apart the faithful for Himself;
the LORD will hear when I call to Him.

PSALM 4:3

This step seems to be fully predictable. As God said to Jeremiah, "Call to me and I will answer you," so we might expect Him to respond to us in the same way. If He is to answer, He must first be listening.

One problem many of us have is that we have difficulty seeing the biblical characters as real people, living and functioning very much in the same way we do. We may even think of them as a breed of spiritual Supermen who, as if coming to earth from another planet, are not limited by human weakness and frailty as we are. But they were special only in the sense—and to the degree—that God chose and equipped and instructed them, and they obeyed Him. Will He work that way with you? Certainly.

Recall the occasion in the book of Acts when, through the apostle Paul, God had healed a crippled man: "When the crowds saw what Paul had done, they raised their voices . . . . 'The gods have come down to us in the form of men!' . . . Then the priest of Zeus . . . with the crowds, intended to offer sacrifice. The apostles Barnabas and Paul tore their robes when they heard this and rushed into the crowd, shouting: 'Men! Why are you doing these things? We are men also, with the same nature as you'" (14:11, 13–15).

First, then, we make the point: God always used ordinary people to accomplish His work on earth. Look at Abraham, Moses, Esther, David, Peter—make your own list. All ordinary people, sinners just like us, but responsive to God's direction—as we desire to be. And, with His help, we can be.

Second, God listened to all of them when they prayed. As human beings, they had the same temptations, weaknesses, and failures that we experience. Yet as contemporary author Dallas Willard writes in his book *Hearing God*: "Our humanity will not by itself prevent us from knowing and interacting with God just as they did."[3]

Lesson: God has chosen to make Himself available to hear us when we pray. Don't blame your humanity for your weakness in prayer. Don't accept your weakness in prayer for *any* reason. God is not limited by our weakness. Our part is to learn to pray as Jesus taught and as He prayed—and to do it as a regular, daily part of our life. This will shape our life as God fills it with Himself in response to our prayers. He will listen, and answer.

Step 3: God Speaks

> *I cry aloud to the* Lord, *and He answers me from*
> *His holy mountain.*
> PSALM 3:4

It is much easier to believe that God *listens* than to accept that He *speaks in response.*

We can certainly believe that He *has* spoken. The Bible is a more-than-adequate record of what He has said, and most of us as Christians are more than ready to believe that He said it all. We may believe even that what He said is right and true. But then we are prone to turn it all into a set of rules and codes of behavior from which we pick and choose the parts we can manage to obey. Not all the parts, mind you, but just enough to keep Him pacified. What an offense that must be to God!

That attitude is proper material for another book. But what we are considering here is this thing called conversational prayer. Granted that God has spoken, does He still speak? And more to the point: Does *He* speak to *me?*

And as a practical matter, does He bring to my mind appropriate truth designed to be applied to my situation, to bring clarity to my confusion, to enable me to make right choices? Yes, He does. The Bible says of itself: "For the word of God is living and effective and sharper than any two-edged sword, penetrating as far as to divide soul, spirit, joints, and marrow; it is a judge of the ideas and thoughts of the heart" (Heb. 4:12). His Word is alive! It is not just ink on paper, to be picked up and then put away at our whim. It is His Word—His way of speaking to us by using our memory to recall it when He wants it to bear His power and deliver His truth! It works in the heart, not merely through the eyes and in the head. (We'll have much more to say about this in part 3 as we consider the vitality and power of incorporating God's Word in our prayers.)

Surely our best guidance comes from God's Word. It is specific, clear, and powerful. But is the Bible the only means of God's communication to us? No indeed. He may use any one of a hundred or a thousand ways. He is not limited by our boundaries.

He will speak to us often through our circumstances. Let me share a personal example to illustrate. When God was making ready to call us into ministry, He first led us to a new job for Jim a thousand miles from where we had lived for thirteen years—only to take the job away one month after we had made the move. In the three years that followed, before we had begun our walk of faith, Jim looked for work in the new city and found none. During those years God was breaking our ties with many of the things that had previously marked our way of life, all the while preparing us to return to our old home with a new direction. Although we had no idea what He was up to, He knew fully what He intended to do with us.

As God works through your circumstances, He may arrange for you to meet certain people, to read certain newspaper stories, to witness some significant event. When you experience a notable change—something you personally did not bring about, or something you started but that took a strange and unpredictable turn—watch to see what God is doing. He may be rearranging your life for a special purpose that only He knows.

Also, God speaks through others in the church, the body of Christ, to give wise counsel or to guide our thinking and our actions. It was a church friend, to whom we showed some of our earlier teaching materials on prayer, who introduced us to the publishers of this and our other books. What seemed a casual meeting, just a cup of coffee between two friends, turned out to be one of the most significant turning points of our lives.

Here's the bottom line: God speaks in any way He chooses. What is most important is not *how* He speaks, but *that* He speaks—and that we be listening. In fact, that is the next component of the prayer process.

Step 4: We Listen

Whether you turn to the right or to the left, your ears will hear a voice behind you, saying, "This is the way; walk in it."
ISAIAH 30:21 NIV

Sometimes God gives what we ask—healing, financial help, or whatever—and our faith is strengthened. At other times, however, it seems that nothing happens. Nothing at all.

But is there nothing at all? Do we measure God's answer only by His action? Is it possible that the answer is coming in the form of a new level of understanding of His purposes in our lives and in the world around us? Or is He taking action that we can't see until He is ready to reveal what He is up to?

Step 4—listening—is surely the difficult, the puzzling, part of prayer. It is unfamiliar territory for most of us. We simply have never been taught to listen when God speaks in response to our prayer. The four-step process can be interrupted, or even stopped, because we may not have understood the true, personal, intimate nature of this relationship that we can have as children of God. He wants to communicate with us. He has given us prayer for this purpose. But *we must want to hear what He says* and believe that He will speak—*to us.*

At a conference years ago, God pierced our hearts when we heard Henry Blackaby lament that many of us pray, but then we go about our day without giving our prayer, or God's response to it, another thought. We all must learn to pray; then we must be attentive and alert to how God may respond. Perhaps it will be through a friend or business associate, a change of plans or direction, a new thought that comes to mind, or an impression that touches our heart. No matter how He sends His message, we must have our spiritual antennae up in order to receive it.

It is our responsibility to listen in order to complete the four-part process of prayer. To be able to hear God's voice is a culmination of all that this book has presented to this point.

Step 5: Our Response

He who belongs to God hears what God says.
JOHN 8:47a NIV

You still may be uncertain as to your ability to hear God when He speaks. Please don't make this a matter of worry or of work. You are not alone. God has given you His Spirit to sharpen your spiritual ears and to open your spiritual eyes. As you become more connected with Him through prayer, and as you grow in your relationship with Him as a natural effect of His Spirit's presence, yielding to Him as you read and obey His Word, and as you commit yourself wholly to living to please Him (as Jesus demonstrated), your ability to hear Him will come. He will see to it. Do your part, and He will do His.

The same God who spoke to Abraham and led him out of Ur; the God who spoke to Moses and led Israel out of Egypt; the God who spoke to David and overcame the Philistine giant, Goliath; the God who rescued Daniel from the lion's den and the three Hebrew boys from the fiery furnace—this same God has sent His Son to die for you, thereby opening the way for you to come to Him with your needs and requests. He is fully able to speak so you can hear, and to demonstrate all His mighty power in and through you as you seek Him with all your heart, coming to Him daily in prayer and listening for His voice.

God said to Moses: "*I will certainly be with you, and this will be the sign to you* that I have sent you: when you bring the people out of Egypt, you will all worship God at this mountain" (Exod. 3:12, emphasis added).

And to Joshua: "No one will be able to stand against you as long as you live. *I will be with you, just as I was with Moses. I will not leave you or forsake you*" (Josh. 1:5, emphasis added).

And to Gideon: "'*But I will be with you,*' the LORD said to him. '*You will strike Midian down as if it were one man*'" (Judg. 6:16, emphasis added).

And to Jeroboam: "After that, if you obey all I command you, walk in My ways, and do what is right in My sight in order to keep My statutes and My commandments as My servant David did, *I will be with you. I will build you a lasting dynasty* just as I built for David, and I will give you Israel" (1 Kings 11:38, emphasis added).

And to His people: "But now thus says the LORD, he who created you, O Jacob, he who formed you, O Israel: 'Fear not, for I have redeemed you; I have called you by name, you are mine. *When you pass through the waters, I will be with you;* and through the rivers, they shall not overwhelm you; when you walk through fire you shall not be burned, and the flame shall not consume you. For I am the LORD your God, the Holy One of Israel, your Savior'" (Isa. 43:1–3 ESV, emphasis added).

So look at it this way: if you're to find the higher ground and live in that intimate relationship you are seeking, you must proceed on the certainty that God is faithful and trustworthy and that He both hears your prayers and answers them. He honors your commitment to pray as you seek to know Him and understand His ways. He knows how to keep your feet on the path He has chosen, and He will reveal the deeper truth as you go.

Step with us now into the realm of Jesus' prayer principles, His teaching, and His example of a life of prayer built upon His relationship with His Father. He is giving us lessons to be learned and applied in our own lives. Higher ground is just ahead.

REFLECTION

Date_____

To Consider: As you think about your prayer life in the past few days or weeks, ask yourself the following questions:

Have there been times when you sensed that you heard God speak to your heart? _____

If yes, what did He impress upon you? _____

_____

_____

_____

If no, how important is it to you that you hear Him? _____

_____

_____

_____

In either case, pause now and write a brief prayer asking God to help you develop a listening ear. Be sure to tell Him that as best you understand your heart, you will obey Him if He asks you to do something. _____

_____

_____

_____

_____

_____

You may want to add this prayer to your own.

Father, I thank You that You are willing to speak to us;
I praise You as our wonderful Shepherd
whose sheep hear Your voice.
Speak clearly to me as You spoke
to Noah, Moses, Elijah, and David,
the man after Your own heart.
Lord, speak to me as You spoke to the woman at the well
and Your disciples on the road to Emmaus.
Help me to be obedient to anything You ask me to do,
and give me the strength and the grace to do it.
In Jesus' name, amen.

Part 2

Jesus' Principles of Prayer

WE MOVE INTO OUR JOURNEY with a fresh view of the hills of higher ground—beginning with the nature of prayer and the reasons Jesus has taught us to pray—as well as the ways. Each hill represents a level of prayer that will lift us in our relationship with God. It will indeed draw us ever closer to Him, not only helping us to understand and respond to more of the deeper truth of who He is, but also of who we are and what our relationship with Him can be—and the difference this relationship makes in the totality of our lives.

Moving Up from Ground Level

More than anything else, the lack of prayer is what keeps us living on ground level. If we're not praying, we're unable to have a personal relationship with God. We can serve without prayer; we can study the Word without it; we can support and care for each other without it; but we cannot know God personally without prayer because it is the primary means by which we build and maintain that relationship. Our relationship with God is developed just as any relationship is formed with any other person (and God is a person)—that is, through spending time with and talking to each other. Prayer allows us to converse with God—speaking, listening, responding. If you have never had that kind of relation-ship with your Lord, don't despair; you can have it. In this book we'll discuss how you can find it, build it, and live in it.

The point we make here is simply that prayer is the essential element of every step we take toward every higher hill that we climb. We can't neglect prayer and expect to ascend higher or draw closer to God.

We Must Be Prepared

When our hearts are stirred toward higher ground, there are some principles we must have in place—some precepts we must grasp—if we are to succeed. Pray right now that God will give you insight and discernment about your own prayer life as you begin part 2.

CHAPTER 5

The Prayer Life of Jesus

Very early in the morning, while it was still dark, Jesus got up, left the house and went off to a solitary place, where he prayed.

MARK 1:35 NIV

Always Our Example

It is the strong, loving hand of Jesus that leads us every step of our journey. He is our leader, our teacher, our model for all that we do in the Christian life. And it is especially important for us to affirm all of this for ourselves as we make upward progress to higher ground. We should be experiencing more of His presence, and thus following the example of His life of prayer.

Remember once more: His life is our life. The life in us and the life in Him is the same life. As we learned from Galatians 2:20, we have died to self and now Christ is living His life in us. This is certainly one of the deep truths of our spiritual life: our new birth in Christ has done away with the old, unchanged life. Now we have entirely new life, and it is the life of Christ, evidenced by the presence of the Holy Spirit within us.

How Does This Impact Your Prayer Life?

It provides both the desire and the power for prayer. It is because Christ's life is in you that your prayers can be heard and answered by the Father, but it is also because of that life that you even have the inclination to pray.

If Christ is our model, our example, we should always watch what He does and take that as the very best way for us as well. So, how did Jesus pray?

The answer is found in simplicity in His prayer in the Garden of Gethsemane: "Yet not as I will, but as You will" (Matt. 26:39). The story is so familiar. Facing death on the cross, Jesus—fully man as well as fully God—spoke to His Father in the agony of the moment: "If it is possible, let this not happen . . . nevertheless, not what I will but what You will."

Jesus' example here becomes even more significant for all of us when we trace the other occasions in His life when that same submission is expressed. Long before the agony of the cross was upon Him, the set of His mind and heart was always to do the Father's will: "I do nothing on My own. But just as the Father taught Me, I say these things. The One who sent Me is with Me. He has not left Me alone, because I always do what pleases Him" (John 8:28–29). This is just one of many such affirmations that Jesus was fully submitted to His Father's will. That is always His prayer, and it is our example. Not my will, Father, but Yours.

How does your prayer life measure up? Is your every prayer, at its heart, a desire for the Father's will to be done? Is self out of the way in your praying? If not, make this a top priority on the hill where God has brought you today—as well as the ones that follow.

Why? Because there is one other aspect of your prayer life that will be strengthened, enriched, and empowered. We deal with this in more detail as we study the Lord's prayer promises in chapter 8, but for now let's have in mind the words of the apostle John concerning prayer that is based upon the will of God: "Now this is the confidence we have before Him: whenever we ask anything according to His will, He hears us. And if we know that He hears whatever we ask, we know that we have what we have asked Him for" (1 John 5:14–15).

Keep this in mind as you contemplate how Jesus prayed and what it can mean when we learn to pray as He prayed. We have whatever we ask when we pray according to the Father's will. If we are fully submitted to Him, in every part of our lives, we will naturally pray that way!

Praying as Jesus Prayed May Take Time

Isn't it amazing how we seem to hurry everything we do? If we can get a hamburger in sixty seconds, why can't we find God's will in about the same amount of time? If Google can give us a long list of resources on any subject in a nanosecond, why can't God?

We are tempted to make our own answer to this question: God can make a squash in three months, but it takes Him one hundred years to grow an oak tree. Most of us, as we approach the higher ground, would rather be an oak than a squash.

The appropriate answer, however, is that God does as He pleases. He is God. Our will must yield to His.

Here again we have Jesus' example to follow. Consider that important occasion—perhaps one of the two or three most important moments of His life—when He was to choose the twelve disciples who would be His closest companions and followers: "During those days He went out to the mountain to pray and spent all night in prayer to God. When daylight came, He summoned His disciples, and He chose 12 of them—He also named them apostles" (Luke 6:12–13).

As we read the full story of Jesus' life in the Gospels, we see that *many* people followed Him (sometimes even called "multitudes"). So what was Jesus doing when He prayed all night? Although we only can speculate, consider that He may not have known which twelve men the Father wanted Him to choose. It may have taken Him all night in prayer to bring many other names and faces before the Father, to be fully instructed in the matter.

That's just speculation, but the fact is that He prayed all night. As we read and meditate on that, we are convicted. Let's face it, most of us have never prayed all night. In fact, there have been many major decisions in our lives about which we prayed not at all. Even now we know that we are prone to make choices that affect our lives and others without spending adequate time in prayer, seeking to hear and understand the Father's will. Shame on us! Let's ask forgiveness, and seek to gain new insight and motivation as we move on to the next hill.

Praying for a Mighty Move of God's Spirit

In our private prayers, both in our homes and in our churches, we pray frequently for God to send revival. We know our nation is under God's remedial judgment. We know that our time is short before He keeps His promise to deal with His own people severely when we ignore His warnings and fail to find and follow His will.

Revival must begin with God's own people, as we frequently recall in quoting from a familiar Old Testament passage: "If

I [God] close the sky so there is no rain, or if I command the grasshopper to consume the land, or if I send pestilence on My people, and My people who are called by My name humble themselves, pray and seek My face, and turn from their evil ways, then I will hear from heaven, forgive their sin, and heal their land. My eyes will now be open and My ears attentive to prayer from this place" (2 Chron. 7:13–15). We often read this passage without really seeing that it is God who closes the sky and commands the grasshopper and sends pestilence *on His own people* when we are disobedient. His judgments always begin with His own people when we fail to be salt and light to a dying world around us.

Praying for revival is urgent in our day, yet we—the people of God—have failed Him and continue to fail Him. This kind of praying is truly praying in agony, something that was also characteristic of Jesus' prayer life. Remember this from Hebrews 5: "During His earthly life, He offered prayers and appeals, with loud cries and tears, to the One who was able to save Him from death, and He was heard because of His reverence. Though a Son, He learned obedience through what He suffered. After He was perfected, He became the source of eternal salvation to all who obey Him" (vv. 7–9).

To pray as Jesus prayed can be painful, but His prayers were heard. Why? Because He was a Son? No, because of His *reverence*—that is, His attitude toward the Father. His prayers were always prayed with an attitude of submission to the greater will of the Father. Surely this kind of praying can take time and can be agonizing. Yet these are the prayers that "avail much" (James 5:16).

As we travel together to the higher ground, remember that this same Lord who prayed in agony and gave up everything for the Father, and who is now calling us to follow Him, also assures us: "Take My yoke upon you and learn from Me, for I am gentle and lowly in heart, and you will find rest for your souls" (Matt. 11:29 NKJV).

In the next chapter we examine the rarely considered process of prayer—the conversation between ourselves and our Lord that is both the substance and the evidence of our relationship with Him. This is truly a step upward to the higher ground—preparation for our adventure into the mind- and spirit-expanding realm of praying God's Word.

REFLECTION

Date_____

To Consider: As you consider Jesus' prayer life and yours, ask yourself these questions:

What impressed you most about Jesus' prayer life, and why?

_____

_____

_____

_____

To what degree are your prayers consciously focused on God's will? _____

_____

_____

_____

If to a high degree, why?_____

_____

_____

If little, again why? _____

_____

_____

Take a moment to write and pray a specific request for God's will to prevail regarding a person or circumstance. Ask God to intervene for His glory._____

_____

_____

_____

_____

_____

You may want to add this prayer to your own.

Father, I come as Jesus came,
to submit my will to You who knows perfectly what is needed
in every life.
You are our Creator God whose hands put the stars in place,
who knows the numbers of hairs on our heads
and when a sparrow falls from a tree—
apart from Your will, not a sparrow falls.
I thank You that Your eye is on the sparrow,
and I rejoice that Your eyes are on me.
Do what is best and right in my life
and in the lives of these for whom I pray,
for I ask in Jesus' name, amen.

CHAPTER 6

Praying as Jesus Taught

We continue our study of Jesus' principles of prayer with a series of six short studies focused on the individual elements of His first recorded teaching on prayer, "the Lord's Prayer" of Matthew 6:9–13.

You may want to use each study as one day's devotional focus during your quiet time. Contemplate what Jesus is teaching us about prayer and what He may be telling us to do as we pray. It is important to recognize the sequence in which He gives the elements of prayer and how each can be a step in your personal journey to higher ground.

Study 1: Moving Higher with *Our Father*

Look now at the first in the series of brief studies from our Lord's basic teaching on prayer. We've kept them short, in every case following up with questions for your personal reflection. Please take the time to thoughtfully, prayerfully answer. Be sure to date your answers so that you can come back to them months or years from now to see how you may have changed and grown. You'll be glad you did.

We've also provided space for you to write and pray a brief but specific prayer, asking God's help in applying each principle in increasingly significant ways in your daily prayer life. The more specific you are, the more able you will be to see God's answers.

Jesus Teaches Us to Pray

Not only has Jesus taught us the importance of daily time with God, but He has shared how we should pray as well: "This, then, is how you should pray" (Matt. 6:9a NIV). That's very clear, isn't it? Note that Jesus doesn't begin to teach *what* we should pray, but *how* we should pray. What follows is what we have traditionally called "The Lord's Prayer," but Jesus isn't giving us specific words to say. Rather, this is a guideline for *the content of our prayer life.* Each day, in our quiet time (even if it's only for a few minutes) and as we move through the day, we should include the elements of prayer that He declared to be essential.

We Acknowledge Our Relationship with God

"Our Father in heaven . . . ."
MATTHEW 6:9b NIV

When Jesus began His model prayer this way, it had huge implications for those listening. In those days, people were not accustomed to referring to God as Father, at least not in a personal family sense of the word. When references to God as Father are found in the Old Testament, the term *father* has more the meaning of "father of the nation," rather than one's personal father.

It's a tremendous privilege that we can address God as our *Father* (a relationship word), showing that we're aware that we belong to Him, that we are His children. (God is not the Father of all human beings, but of those who come to Him through faith in Jesus Christ [see John 1:12].) When we consider what it means to be His children, how grateful should we be?

This is so important that surely it's worth a moment's reflection before we continue.

* * * * *

As part of the same sermon, Jesus helps us understand what it means to be able to come to God as our Father: "What man among you, if his son asks him for bread, will give him a stone? Or if he asks for a fish, will give him a snake? If you then, who are evil, know how to give good gifts to your children, how much more will your Father in heaven give good things to those who ask Him!" (Matt. 7:9–11). God is our loving Father, who is eager to give good things to His dependent children. We should come to Him with an attitude of humble expectancy that He will hear and answer our prayers in the best way, for our good and for His glory. These are things that we should contemplate and be grateful for as we begin our time of prayer.

Study 2: Moving Higher through *Worship*
We Worship Our Father

> *"[H]allowed be your name . . . ."*
> MATTHEW 6:9b NIV

We hallow (or honor) God's name with our personal worship—simple, heartfelt words of honor and praise for who He is and what He means to us. This doesn't have to be a lengthy time of worship, but one that is from the heart. Clearly, by Jesus' teaching here, we're to worship God *before* we ask Him for anything.

We worship Him when we pause to reflect on who He is and how He works in the world, truth that is revealed throughout the Bible. The more familiar we are with the Word of God, the more we learn about Him, which tells us the myriad ways we can come to know Him. We've just reflected on the fact that

He is our Father, willing to give more of His generosity and His love than any earthly father could. These meditations of our heart become worship when expressed in prayer.

Father, Abba Father, I worship You
as One who loves me perfectly, just as I am.
I praise You as my Father, who is willing to give me Your best,
to answer my prayers in a way
that best reflects Your love and exceeds my expectations!

We might also think of Him, even briefly, as our faithful God (1 Cor. 1:9), who has promised never to leave us or forsake us (Heb. 13:5). What an incredible promise! How worthy of worship is the God who makes such a promise! What ramifications does it have for our lives? We will never be alone! Can our hearts not break into praise at such truth? Such spontaneous, personal worship, expressed in prayer, is pleasing and honoring to God, and it takes only a moment.

How I worship You, Abba Father,
as my faithful God!
I praise You for Your faithfulness
and I rejoice in the truth
that You will never leave me, never forsake me,
that I'll never have to face one day of life without You!

This is what is meant by *hallowing God's name.* His name represents who He is—His character and nature, His attributes. There are literally hundreds of such names and attributes in Scripture, and the more we read of them and think about them, the more they become ingrained in our hearts and minds so that they become a natural part of our prayers and worship. They reveal the deeper truths not only of who God is but of the countless ways He is willing to reveal Himself to us, to respond to us at any point in our lives. We can't have a well-rounded, complete view and understanding of who God is and who He wants to be for us—engaged and involved in our lives—apart from His Word.

Study 3: Moving Higher through *Surrender*
We Surrender Our Lives

> *"Your kingdom come. Your will be done*
> *on earth as it is in heaven."*
> MATTHEW 6:10

In one sense we are asking for God's kingdom to come here on earth, as we know it one day will. But Jesus taught many different things about the kingdom, one being that "the kingdom of God is within you" (Luke 17:21 NIV). It is the King who rules the kingdom, and if the kingdom of God is within us, the King is the one in charge. Our King is Jesus (Matt. 25:34), our King of kings and Lord of lords (1 Tim. 6:15).

But how does He live within us? Through the Holy Spirit, the gift all believers have received (Acts 1:8), the One who lives in us: "And I will ask the Father, and he will give you another Counselor to be with you forever—the Spirit of truth. The world cannot accept him, because it neither sees him nor knows him. But you know him, for he lives with you and will be in you" (John 14:16–18 NIV). The Holy Spirit—the Counselor—is also known as the Spirit of Jesus (Acts 16:7; Phil. 1:19).

We know that the Spirit lives within us if we have received Christ, but Scripture tells us that we can quench or stifle the Spirit within (1 Thess. 5:19), and Paul commands us to be filled with the Spirit (Eph. 5:18). We've already discussed Jesus' admonition that we're to deny ourselves (Luke 9:23), so what conclusion can we draw from this? The Holy Spirit lives within us, but He cannot totally fill us or rule in our lives if we haven't denied ourselves. We must become less so that He can become more (John 3:30). We can't be filled with self and also be filled with the Spirit. Self is what quenches the Spirit and stifles His presence, limiting His influence in our lives. Jesus is saying here that at the onset of our daily prayers, as we have rejoiced in our relationship with our heavenly Father, as we have offered Him our worship and praise, we must humble ourselves through surrender, giving up self to His right to rule in our lives.

The words are simple—*Lord, I give You my life.* But saying it is not always easy because full surrender means completely letting go, choosing to hold on to *nothing*—not family, home, business, career, church, goals, dreams, etc. For most of us, this process of letting go is realized gradually, sometimes taking years because we don't even see what we're holding back. Status? Image? Comfort? Security? Time? He wants it all (Luke 14:33). Do you verbalize that in your prayers? Do you ever ask, *Is there anything I've not surrendered?* Tough question.

Personally, we remember confronting the issue of surrender early on in our ministry. I, Jim, was being considered to manage a newly forming Christian radio network in Romania, a commitment that would require our living there for three to five years. I was one of the final three candidates, and we felt it likely I was going to be chosen. We had to lay everything on the line to say to the Lord, yes, we're willing to go. And though it was a struggle, especially for Kaye, we put everything on the altar: lifestyle, family, grandchildren, etc. Yet once we had, someone else was selected for the position. We both sensed that it had been a test, like putting Isaac on the altar had been for Abraham (Gen. 22:1–14).

Remember, we are talking about the higher ground of the personal relationship with Almighty God. The deeper truth is that He is the King, and we are His servants. It is only as we are fully surrendered that He can fill us with His Spirit and best accomplish His kingdom work in and through us. The less of us, the more of Him! In our daily prayers we are to acknowledge that He is our King and the Lord of our lives, and we surrender our lives to Him, asking that His will, not ours, be done.

Study 4: Moving Higher through *Supplication*
We Ask for What We Need

"Give us today our daily bread."
MATTHEW 6:11

Have you noted that Jesus prefaced supplication (asking) with worship and surrender? This is a significant point. How often do most of us rush into God's presence with "Help me . . ." or, "I need . . ." In His model prayer, Jesus shows us that such prayers are important and necessary, but it's our worship and surrender that reveal the attitude of our hearts. When we begin our prayer time with even a brief outpouring of worship, it must please God, for He seeks those who will worship Him (John 4:23)!

By coming to God every day—note the petition for *daily* bread—for basic essentials that we need, we are affirming our utter dependence upon Him. We are not presuming; we are acknowledging that He is God our Provider and we need Him. Our worship already has shown that we need Him not merely for what He can give us or do for us but because of who He is. It's this childlike dependence that sets the stage for His giving nature to respond. As we've already seen, He wants to give far more than we ask.

Our asking daily is important because, as we learn from James, "You do not have because you do not ask. You ask and don't receive because you ask wrongly, so that you may spend it on your desires for pleasure" (James 4:2b–3). If we don't ask, we may not receive what we need. Did you note James's reference to motives? If we ask with wrong motives, wanting something primarily for our own selfish pleasure, God doesn't answer. This doesn't mean God won't give us things for our pleasure; He just doesn't want that to be our motive. He wants it to be His gift to His humble child.

We Can Pray at Any Time, from Any Place

We've said that the model prayer we're discussing includes elements of prayer that do not always have to be prayed in the quiet time, although that's the best time for us to be still and listen for God's direction and coaching as we pray. But as a practical matter, we often find ourselves praying as we move through the busyness of our days. May we suggest that the effectiveness of those prayers is directly related to the quiet-time prayers of worship, surrender, and confession of sins (which we'll be discussing next)? Let us give you an example from Nehemiah:

> When I [Nehemiah] heard these words [that the wall of Jerusalem was broken down], I sat down and wept. I mourned for a number of days, fasting and praying before the God of heaven. I said, LORD God of heaven, the great and awe-inspiring God who keeps His gracious covenant with those who love Him and keep His commands *[worship, hallowing His name]*, let Your eyes be open and Your ears be attentive to hear Your servant's *[surrender]* prayer. . . . I confess

the sins we have committed against You. Both I and my father's house have sinned *[confession]*. . . . Please, Lord, let Your ear be attentive to the prayer of Your servant and to that of Your servants who delight to revere Your name. Give Your servant success today, and have compassion on him in the presence of this man. At the time, I was the king's cupbearer. (Neh. 1:4–11)

I [Nehemiah] took the wine and gave it to the king. I had never been sad in his presence, so the king said to me, "Why are you sad, when you aren't sick? . . . I was overwhelmed with fear and replied to the king, "May the king live forever! Why should I not be sad when the city where my ancestors are buried lies in ruins and its gates have been destroyed by fire?" Then the king asked me, "What is your request?" *So I prayed to the God of heaven* and answered the king, "If it pleases the king, and if your servant has found favor with you, send me to Judah and to the city where my ancestors are buried, so that I may rebuild it." The king . . . asked me, "How long will your journey take, and when will you return?" So I gave him a definite time, and it pleased the king to send me." (Neh. 2:1–6, notes and emphasis added)

Nehemiah had a powerful personal prayer life. In the above recorded prayer, we've noted that he was a man who worshipped God, hallowing His name; who surrendered to God as His servant; and who confessed his sins—then he asked for favor with the king. He prayed as Jesus taught. He didn't rush into God's presence in the busyness of his duties with the king and call out for God's favor; he had prepared in advance.

So it is with us. If we spend even a few minutes at the beginning of the day to worship, surrender, and confess our sins, we will have prepared the way for supplication as we go through the day.

God Doesn't Always Answer Prayers Right Away

This isn't news to anyone, is it? We've all known people who have prayed for many years before God answered. In fact, we have, and perhaps you have too.

Sometimes God doesn't answer because He knows that what we've asked for isn't the right thing. Sometimes it is simply that He wants to give us something different, something better. Often it's a question of timing, and His timing is always right. Perhaps it is a matter of building our character so we're able to handle what He wants to give us. Sometimes God is saying no, as He said to Paul who asked three times that the thorn be removed from his flesh (2 Cor. 12:7–9). Why do you think Paul was able to hear the Lord so clearly? What kind of relationship did Paul have with the Lord?

God will as surely direct our prayers when we are living on the higher ground of intimacy with Him. We'll be able to discern His voice (1 Kings 19:12) and know His will. The point is, we're to ask. Jesus said we should ask for what we need.

Study 5: Moving Higher through *Confession*

As we take the principles of the Lord's Prayer as a beginning point for learning to pray as Jesus taught, keep in mind that even though we are encouraging you to include these different principles of prayer in your daily prayer life, they need not be long prayers. God doesn't need a lot of words from us; He looks on our hearts. But there are some words He does want to hear.

We Confess Our Sins

"And forgive us our debts [sins] . . . ."
MATTHEW 6:12a

As Christians, we recognize that we are sinners and need to be forgiven, and that we must ask forgiveness for our sins, our disobedience, and our failure to obey the commands and principles of His Word for our lives. In our daily prayer time, we must take this into account if we want to live in the fullness of a personal relationship with God. The Bible tells us that if we hold on to sin our prayers may be hindered (1 Pet. 3:7); God may choose not to hear (Isa. 59:2; Ps. 66:18). In His model prayer, Jesus is saying, in effect, that we should be keeping short accounts with God—we should confess specific sins as we become aware of them. We recommend that you always pause in your prayers to ask God if there is something you should confess that you are not aware of. (Most of us are masters at rationalizing or explaining away our sins, overlooking or conveniently forgetting them.)

We Forgive Others

"[A]s we also have forgiven our debtors"
[those who sin against us].
MATTHEW 6:12b

The last half of this verse is the most difficult part of the prayer for many Christians. We're not only to ask forgiveness for our sins, we are to forgive others for the wrongs that are done to us. The seriousness of this command is emphasized later (Matt. 6:14–15) as Jesus declares that we must forgive others *if we expect to be forgiven.* This is especially pertinent to our discussion of the higher ground of intimacy with God, because that is what Jesus is referring to. He doesn't mean that our salvation is at risk; all our sins (Col. 2:13)—past, present, and future—have been forgiven. But God is a holy God, and before we enter His presence, we must confess and be cleansed of sin: "If we say, 'We have no sin,' we are deceiving ourselves, and the truth is not in us. If we confess our sins, He is faithful and righteous to forgive us our sins and to cleanse us from all unrighteousness" (1 John 1:8–9).

Unforgiveness is a sin that must be forgiven and cleansed if we are to enjoy the higher ground with our Father. The good thing is, with unforgiveness or any other sin, if we confess with sincere hearts, He is faithful and righteous to forgive us and cleanse us. Forgiving others is a choice we make—out of obedience to God—not an emotion. We don't have to feel like forgiving; we simply must do it if we want to come higher. A deeper truth is that unforgiveness is a sin that is destructive to our attitudes and relationships even beyond the person we need to forgive. We hurt only ourselves when we cling to this sin.

Study 6: Moving Higher through *Testing and Deliverance*
We Ask Not to Be Put to the Test

"And do not bring us into temptation . . . ."

MATTHEW 6:13a

The word used for temptation means "testing." Sometimes the test is not clearly a matter of right and wrong, but of the temptation to pursue the good in lieu of the best. It's often Satan's way to get us slightly off track—just enough to keep us from finding God's best in our lives. We pray to be delivered from that kind of testing because we can easily be set back in our progress toward spiritual maturity by the interruption that such a test can bring. It's interesting that Jesus presents this principle immediately following the prayer of confession and forgiveness. We ask not to be put to the test while the sorrow over the failures we've just confessed is fresh in our minds. The deeper truth might be insight to pray about those areas of specific testing, asking to avoid further tests until He knows we're strong enough to resist and have victory.

We Ask for Protection from Satan

"[B]ut deliver us from the evil one."
MATTHEW 6:13b

The word that is translated "evil one" is masculine, not neuter, referring to Satan, not some "cosmic power of evil." Satan is alive and "prowling around like a roaring lion" (1 Pet. 5:8b), and we're told here to ask God to protect us from him. If you are not in the habit of asking for this protection daily, we urge you to take this principle seriously, especially as you are seeking higher ground. Satan isn't pleased when we grow in our prayer lives and become more powerful and effective in our prayers—which will happen as a result of living on the higher ground where we spend more time in prayer and fellowship with our Father, where we take on more issues in our lives and become more like Christ, more filled with His Spirit. We don't need to be fearful of Satan, but we do need to be vigilant and aware.

Keep in mind, too, that Satan isn't always responsible for the things that go wrong in our lives. We have not one enemy but three—the world, the flesh (self), and the devil. Of the three, self is much more likely to cause us problems than Satan; much of what we deal with is the consequence of sins. One reason it's important to confess our sins and be willing to repent, or turn away from them in God's strength, is as Paul teaches us: "Therefore each of you must put off falsehood and speak truthfully to his neighbor, for we are all members of one body. 'In your anger do not sin': Do not let the sun go down while you are still angry, and *do not give the devil a foothold.* He who has been stealing must steal no longer, but must work, doing something useful with his own hands, that he may have something to share with those in need" (Eph. 4:25–28 NIV, emphasis added). "Do not give the devil a foothold" also can be translated "Don't give the devil an opportunity." Note that in the above quote several sins are mentioned; and in the larger context of this chapter, there are even more sins named. Paul is stating a principle: if we let the sun go down without confessing our sins, we are giving the devil an opportunity to influence us in some way, perhaps even to gain control over that part of our lives. We don't want that.

REFLECTION

Date_____

To Consider: As you think about your prayer life in the past few days or weeks, ask these questions:

Do you ever rush into God's presence without pausing to reflect on the tremendous privilege He has given you? _____

_____

Is personal worship always or generally a part of your prayer life?

_____

_____

Are you in the habit of pausing to worship or praise God as you begin prayer? _____

_____

If yes, in what way do you feel this prepares your heart? _____

_____

_____

_____

Have you verbalized your desire to surrender everything to the Lord? _____

Are you aware of anything you have not surrendered?_____

_____

What are the things you typically ask God for?_____

_____

_____

_____

Are you specific in your prayers?_____

_____

If so, give examples. _____

_____

_____

_____

If not, how do you know when you see answers? _____

_____

Have you been thoughtful and specific in confessing sins? ____

_____

Is there someone you have not forgiven? _____

_____

Is it your habit to pray for protection from the evil one every
day? _____

_____

How important do you think it is to pray this way, and why?

_____

_____

_____

_____

Are you aware of sins that you have not confessed, that you may
have let the sun go down on? If so, pause and take care of that
right now._____

_____

_____

You may want to add this prayer to your own.

> *Father, I praise You that You are my*
> *Defender, Protector, Stronghold, and Shield,*
> *One who surrounds me like the mountains surround Jerusalem.*
> *You are the Lord of Hosts,*
> *the Commander of the armies of heaven—*
> *if You are for us, who can be against us?*
> *Holy Shepherd,*
> *who protects me with Your rod and staff,*
> *keep me free from the influence of the evil one.*
> *I pray in Jesus' name, amen.*

CHAPTER 7

Two Prayer Parables

While the model prayer of Matthew 6:9–13 must be seen as our Lord's first, elementary, and most comprehensive teaching on prayer—and deserves all the books written to analyze and honor it—it is not everything He had to say on the subject. Two of His later parables contain truth and instruction appropriate for those disciples who had walked with Him daily for some eighteen months after hearing the Sermon on the Mount. Because these parables represent later teaching (therefore, teaching for followers who were in a different state of mind and at a different stage of spiritual growth), they can be seen together as addressing a need that Jesus recognized in the lives of these men.

The Importance of Intercessory Prayer

In Luke 11 we have a record of our Lord's second teaching of that model prayer. The chapter begins as the disciples, having seen Jesus praying (one of how many such times?), ask Him to teach them to pray (a point we dealt with in chap. 1). As we might expect, Jesus responded with the same essential teaching He had given in the Sermon on the Mount (Matt. 6:9–13).

Now Jesus adds more to their understanding of prayer through the parable that we know as the Friend at Midnight:

"He also said to them: 'Suppose one of you has a friend and goes to him at midnight and says to him, "Friend, lend me three loaves of bread, because a friend of mine on a journey has come to me, and I don't have anything to offer him." Then he will answer from inside and say, "Don't bother me! The door is already locked, and my children and I have gone to bed. I can't get up to give you anything." I tell you, even though he won't get up and give him anything because he is his friend, yet because of his persistence, he will get up and give him as much as he needs'" (Luke 11:5–8). Here we have Jesus' only specific teaching on the subject of intercessory prayer—which simply means praying on behalf of others.

The story is familiar, but the circumstances may be strange to us—and the drama of it is worth our attention. The Wycliffe Bible Commentary helps us to better understand the setting: "The . . . parable was given by Jesus to illustrate the certainty of answer to prayer. In it he placed prayer on the basis of personal friendship with God. *Midnight.* The most dangerous and inconvenient hour for a call. People in our Lord's day seldom ventured out at night for fear of bandits. A friend . . . in his journey is come. If the friend traveled on foot all day, and did not arrive until midnight, he must have been desperately hungry. Hospitality demanded that he be fed."[1]

Our Lord tells His story with three characters. A man who knocks on the door of a friend at midnight. The friend, desiring to follow the propriety of that day, wants to offer a meal. He has no bread to give him, but he admits the traveler, then goes to a neighbor's house and knocks on the door seeking bread. The neighbor, not wanting to get out of bed, declines to respond. But after repeated pounding on the door, the mission is accomplished; the neighbor gets up and gives the bread and the man is fed.

We best understand the scope of the parable, and capture its meaning, as we borrow from a very clear analysis by Andrew Murray in his book *The Ministry of Intercession.*[2]

The lesson that Jesus was teaching has to do with the elements that are involved when we are called to engage in true intercession. They are:

- *An urgent need.* The man was hungry and came asking for help. When we examine the nature of our own intercessions on behalf of friends, family, and others, we can agree that this is always the beginning of intercessory prayer. If the need is not urgent, we probably don't bother to pray.

- *A willing love.* It takes a lot of love to get up at midnight and open the door for a hungry man when you have no bread to give him. In the same way, we realize that when it comes to meeting the deepest needs of others, we have no "bread" to give.

- *A sense of helplessness.* We simply cannot save a soul, or heal a disease, or restore a marriage. Sometimes we can give some money, or some advice, or some sympathy, but we really cannot solve the problem. The bottom line, always, is that we really cannot give the kind of help that is needed.

- *Faith in prayer.* Though the man had no bread to give, he knew where bread could be found. His neighbor had bread, and he set out to do what he could to help the hungry friend. That's our position when we meet someone in real need. We have no bread, but we know who does. And we know that when we ask Him, we will be heard and answered.

- *Perseverance.* The first knock didn't bring results, but perseverance paid off. The man kept knocking until the neighbor responded. The lesson here is not that God is reluctant to give what we ask, but that He wants to see how important the prayer is to us. He already knows the need, and God never has to be pressed to action. But are we willing to keep on praying until the answer comes? That is the point.

- *A rich reward.* The bread was given. The hunger was satisfied. The prayer was answered, and faith was strengthened.

Keep this lesson in mind as you undertake to pray for someone in need. Share it with your prayer group. Encourage all who pray to continue until God answers—either giving what you ask or showing you that the need for the prayer is over. Again, it is not a matter of forcing God's hand; we are incapable of that. But He is very interested in the progress of our prayer life.

As evidence of the last point, look at the next verses in which Jesus reinforces all that He has taught in this vital parable: "So I say to you, keep asking, and it will be given to you. Keep searching, and you will find. Keep knocking, and the door will be opened to you. For everyone who asks receives, and the one who searches finds, and to the one who knocks, the door will be opened. What father among you, if his son asks for a fish, will give him a snake instead of a fish? Or if he asks for an egg, will give him a scorpion? If you then, who are evil, know how to give good gifts to your children, how much more will the heavenly Father give the Holy Spirit to those who ask Him?" (Luke 11:9–13).

What an encouragement we find in Luke 11:1–8! The Master Teacher reminds us of the necessary elements of our life of prayer, focuses on the friendship of the Father, and shines new light on the urgency of both compassion and persistence as we intercede for the deep needs of others.

Boldness in Prayer

The second parable Jesus chose for a higher level of prayer instruction is found in Luke 18: "He then told them a parable on the need for them to pray always and not become discouraged: 'There was a judge in one town who didn't fear God or respect man. And a widow in that town kept coming to him, saying, "Give me justice against my adversary." For a while he was unwilling, but later he said to himself, "Even though I don't fear God or respect man, yet because this widow keeps pestering me, I will give her justice, so she doesn't wear me out by her persistent coming."' Then the Lord said, 'Listen to what the unjust judge says. Will not God grant justice to His elect who cry out to Him day and night? Will He delay to help them? I tell you that He will swiftly grant them justice'" (vv. 1–8a).

The lessons of the two parables are similar, but not quite the same. Persistence is obviously a factor in both, but here it seems that the element of *boldness* is preeminent. It takes a great deal of love and courage to do what the Friend at Midnight did, but how much more boldness would be required to keep going back to a judge who refused to hear your plea? Judges, as a rule, don't take kindly to impertinence and irritation.

But the widow knew she had a right to ask for justice, and she was determined.

In the same way, Jesus instructs His disciples to understand that they (and we) have a right to plead our cause before Almighty God. The lesson, as Luke reports, is that we are to "pray always and not become discouraged."

Are weariness and discouragement problems for you in your intercessory praying? Do you often wish God would hurry up and take care of the matter? We're impatient people, and we tend to give up when something doesn't work as we want it to right away.

Lessons from the Lips of Jesus

Consider the gracious method of our Lord in dealing with His disciples. He has taught them how to pray and has reinforced that teaching. They have walked with Him for most of two years, and He was aware that He would not always be with them to guide their thinking. They have seen Him praying and recognized that it was in Jesus' prayer life that He gained wisdom from the Father and strength for the difficult life that He was now leading. They wanted to learn to pray, and He was more than ready to teach them.

So here they are—moving to a higher hill in their relationship to Him. He knows that each next hill requires and justifies new learning and new understanding. Soon they will be on their own. He will send the Holy Spirit to remind them of all He has told them, but He Himself will be gone.

The time had come. They must be helped to grow, to come up higher. This is higher ground for them, and deeper truth. This is more than just teaching the disciples *how to pray*; Jesus was teaching them how to view the life of prayer so that God's purposes could be accomplished through this group of individuals who would be responsible for building His church. He lifted them to a level from which further growth would be possible.

These are vital life lessons for all of us. If we are to find the deep and personal relationship with our Father that we desire—which is the purpose of our journey to higher ground—it will be important for us to note how our Lord dealt with those earlier disciples. He will deal with us in the same way. We must be prepared to grow to maturity in our prayer lives, not remain satisfied with the basics. He is teaching us to come up higher, and we must.

REFLECTION

Date_____

To Consider: Read the parables again, direct from your Bible, and ask yourself:

In your own life, have you been faced with meeting a desperate need of a friend? Recall it here. _____

_____

_____

_____

How did you respond? _____

_____

_____

_____

Did you pray and find God faithful to answer? _____

If not, what do you think was missing?_____

_____

_____

Have you experienced the need for persistence and boldness in your own prayer life? Explain. _____

_____

_____

_____

Pause now, and ask God to show you how this teaching of Jesus might equip you in your journey to higher ground with Him.

_____

_____

_____

_____

_____

_____

_____

You may want to add this prayer to your own.

Father, I know that my prayers have often been hindered
by my own weakness and uncertainty,
for You are all-powerful, able to meet every need.
May I, like the Friend at Midnight, be ready at any moment
to bring the needs of others to You boldly,
to stand in the gap for those who are not able to come on their own.
Help me to lay self aside, and in love—
with the compassion of Christ—
knock on the door of Your heart and keep on knocking,
in order that You may bestow the blessings,
the healing,
the provision
that others need, and for which they seek my help.
I pray this in the name of my Lord, my Savior,
Jesus Christ the King, amen.

CHAPTER 8

Understanding Jesus' Prayer Promises

*God is not a man, that he should lie, nor a son of man,
that he should change his mind. Does he speak and then not act?
Does he promise and not fulfill?*

NUMBERS 23:19 NIV

As we move from hill to higher hill, we're also moving from truth to truth, seeking to fortify our minds as well as thrill our hearts with the prospect of a life-affirming relationship with God.

At each new level, it is important that we gain knowledge that builds upon the foundation that was our ground-level starting point. One thing we need is the ability to dispel misconceptions—things that have led many, Christian and non-Christian, to expectations that are both unbiblical and unrealistic.

A Closer Look

Jesus has made some astounding, amazing, thrilling promises. For example, He says plainly that His disciples—and that includes us—can have whatever we ask in prayer. Taken out of context, these promises may sound like blank checks, ready to be cashed for whatever blessing we want from God.

94

We have a good friend whose life is devoted to prison ministry. In fact, it was Frank who invited us to work with him in a maximum-security men's prison early in our own ministry—with the result that we produced our first group study on prayer. A group of forty men, believers behind bars, were meeting every Thursday for an hour to pray. The chaplain asked us to teach them to pray, just as Jesus had been teaching us. And we did.

That was ten years ago. Recently Frank came to us with a question. An inmate, a new Christian, had just presented his appeal before the parole board for consideration of possible release. Reading his Bible regularly, as any eager new Christian would do, he had found those promises where Jesus says we can ask anything in His name and He will do it. "I prayed," said the inmate, "and asked in Jesus' name that I would get my parole. Then they turned me down. I don't understand. Why?"

The question may be simplistic, and we veteran believers should know the answer, at least in a way that satisfies us. But it is amazing how many Christians, who should be mature and knowledgeable in the Scriptures, can be tangled up by such questions.

To Whom Are Jesus' Promises Made?

Herein lies the most basic answer to the prison inmate's question—and, in fact, to many questions that arise about biblical statements. In every case, we need to know, as specifically as possible, to whom the promises were made.

Jesus' prayer promises are made to the disciples, not to the crowds—not to the unbelieving, doubting, hostile leaders or to the mobs that confronted Him in His ministry. He intended (and now intends) these promises for the equipping of His disciples. And for what was He equipping them? For their assignment of establishing His church on earth, for the building of His kingdom, and (in at least one case) to teach a valuable lesson for kingdom life and service.

Are these promises for us? Yes, as we meet His qualifications for discipleship. That should be the answer to the inmate's question. The promise was made to eleven men who had walked daily with Jesus, learned from Him, and were ready to lay down their lives for Him—to be martyred if need be. And martyrdom did indeed await those men, all except one, as history reports it. While, in that upper room, they still did not fully understand all His cross would reveal, their hearts were fully His.

What did Jesus say in Matthew 16:24? A disciple is one who denies self, takes up a cross (choosing to die to whatever may interfere in our relationship with Him), and follows Jesus in obedience to His commands. When we have met those requirements, certainly the promises are for us too. Stripped of our self-interest, self-promotion, self-exaltation (and all the other "self" things), we can have whatever we ask. But note: we'll not ask for unworthy things. We will ask that God's will be done in all circumstances and that we will be instruments in the carrying out of His purposes.

This can be a fact of our life as we move to the higher ground. On which next hill will we find it? That is pretty much up to us and the choices we make in response to His continuing revelation of the deeper truth. Matthew 16:24 *is* deeper truth, and its meaning is quite clear.

There Are Conditions and Lessons to Be Learned

We need to look now at the content of Jesus' promises from three perspectives that our knowledge of God's Word will affirm:

- Jesus means exactly what He says when He makes promises. There is no "catch 22."
- The promises are sometimes designed to teach spiritual lessons, like the parables.
- The promises have conditions attached—and the conditions are not tricks that allow our Lord to smile and say "Gotcha!"

Let's examine some of the promises as they appear in the Gospel accounts.

A Kingdom Promise. To keep our discussion in proper sequence, let's begin with the promise that we find in Matthew 7. In His Sermon on the Mount, Jesus has been laying down the standards of life in His kingdom. He has given the disciples the basic teaching on prayer in chapter 6 (The Lord's Prayer). Now, in chapter 7, He follows with the benefit that comes through prayer for those who are living according to His criteria for life in His kingdom (the kingdom of the heart and spirit, with Himself ruling and reigning): "Keep asking, and it will be given to you. Keep searching, and you will find. Keep knocking, and the door will be opened to you. For everyone who asks receives, and the one who searches finds, and to the one who knocks, the door will be opened. What man among you, if his son asks him for bread, will give him a stone? Or if he asks for a fish, will give him a snake? If you then, who are evil, know how to give good gifts to your children, how much more will your Father in heaven give good things to those who ask Him!" (Matt. 7:7–11).

The Sermon on the Mount presents everything within the context of its main purpose—to make clear what Jesus intends to be the lifestyle, the character, the image, and the benefits of citizenship in His kingdom. The promise of Matthew 7:7, then, is for those who live obedient, submissive lives as the Sermon requires. It is not for the unbeliever, and it is not for the disobedient. It is for those who desire to live on higher ground, who are willing to remain in fellowship with the Master.

An Instructive Promise. A second prayer promise is of a different character entirely. It is a promise that Jesus gives to His disciples to assure them of the power of the prayer of faith and its effect in the realm of prayer. In Mark 11, Jesus has entered Jerusalem in preparation for His final days prior to the cross. The disciples have just seen one of His most puzzling acts—the cursing of a fig tree, representing the failure of Israel to obey God and bear the fruit that God intended. He tells the disciples, who not only are amazed at His power over nature, but are wondering about the significance of the act itself: "'Have faith in God,' Jesus answered. 'I tell you the truth, if anyone says to this mountain, "Go, throw yourself into the sea," and does not doubt in his heart but believes that what he says will happen, it will be done for him. Therefore I tell you, whatever you ask for in prayer, believe that you have received it, and it will be yours. And when you stand praying, if you hold anything against anyone, forgive him, so that your Father in heaven may forgive you your sins'" (Mark 11:22–25 NIV).

This is a *teaching* promise. The mountain, in Scripture, is usually symbolic of great difficulty. Jesus often made the point that our faith must be in God, whose unlimited power is ours as we trust Him completely. The promise is that the God who is almighty can and will give all the power that is needed for any task. Moving mountains is not a necessary aspect of the disciple's life, but the power to move mountains—*and the power to forgive sins*—is in God, who knows what we really need and responds when we ask, believing.

A Promise about United Prayer. Another significant promise is found in yet a different context. In Matthew 18, Jesus has just taught the disciples how to deal with a brother who sins against another brother. The underlying truth is about the authority that God has given to His gathered people in what would become known as the *ekklesia,* the called-out people, the church. We are to deal with sinning brothers and sisters by a certain pattern given by Jesus in this chapter.

It is here that the Lord gives a promise concerning the power of His earthly body through united prayer: "If two of you on earth agree about any matter that you pray for, it will be done for you by My Father in heaven. For where two or three are gathered together in My name, I am there among them" (Matt. 18:19–20). As we look carefully, we find that there are three elements upon which this promise rests.

The first is *agreement* concerning what we are asking with united hearts. The promise is for the church—even in its smallest group cluster. It isn't enough simply to get together and say "I agree" to something one person may ask. In the context, Jesus is saying that the promise pertains to prayer for kingdom purposes, and it also must involve a second element: *gathering in the name of Jesus.* His name must be the bond, the thing that holds us together when we pray. To meet in His name is to have Him present. If He is present, He is able to lift our prayers to the Father for action.

The third element is *the certainty of an answer*: "It will be done for you by my Father in heaven." If we agree, and gather in His name, the answer will come (not always as we wish, but as God knows best). In the unity of faith, the power of the name and the presence of Jesus are in control, and the answer comes. The evidence that there has been true, united prayer is the answer; we receive what we asked for.

Promises in the Upper Room

Perhaps the most memorable prayer promises are those we find in Jesus' conversation with His disciples in the Upper Room on the last night of His earthly life and ministry. Let's look at the first four, one at a time, as the apostle John reports them in his Gospel, chapters 14 through 16.

> "I assure you: The one who believes in Me will also do the works that I do. And he will do even greater works than these, because I am going to the Father. Whatever you ask in My name, I will do it so that the Father may be glorified in the Son. If you ask Me anything in My name, I will do it." (John 14:12–14)

Do you hear the Lord's condition here? If so, you will want to make a practice of asking yourself this question: *If God hears and answers the prayer I am now praying, will it bring glory to Him?* That is precisely what Jesus was saying. He would do whatever they asked, because in that process the Father would be glorified. There is no hint that He would provide a nicer house, or a younger donkey, or the right woman for a wife. Those are not the things that were at issue on that evening. And, on the higher ground, they will become less and less important to us as well.

> "If you remain in Me and My words remain in you, ask whatever you want and it will be done for you. My Father is glorified by this: that you produce much fruit and prove to be My disciples." (John 15:7–8)

The condition here is in the form of an "if." Jesus says, "*If* you remain [abide] in Me, and *[if]* My words [my teachings, my commands, my assignments] remain in you. . . ." And then He adds a purpose for the promise: that the disciples would produce much fruit—with the result, again, that the Father is glorified. The fruit is lives changed, the church strengthened, the kingdom established, Christ lifted up before the world. These should be the results of our service as disciples, and they bring glory to God.

So this promise has to do with their response to Him and to their lives under the headship of the Father in heaven. These, He says, are the real tests as to whether these men are or are not His disciples. Can we meet the test? The fellowship with the Father and the Son on the higher ground will bring many changes. This is deep truth.

> "You did not choose Me, but I chose you. I
> appointed you that you should go out and produce
> fruit and that your fruit should remain, so that what-
> ever you ask the Father in My name, He will give
> you. This is what I command you: love one another."
> (John 15:16–17)

Two things get our attention in this one. Fruit, again— a part of His analogy of Himself as the true Vine and of us (disciples) as the branches. The fruit comes to the branches, not the vine. But the life comes through the vine to the branches. It is a link that must be maintained. That is what these promises are illustrating. It is *relationship*—just what we're after on the higher ground, is it not? And here He adds one more thing— the command that we disciples love one another. There must be love between members in the body of Christ, and in all its manifestations, if we are to claim these promises.

> "I assure you: Anything you ask the Father in My
> name, He will give you. Until now you have asked for
> nothing in My name. Ask and you will receive, that
> your joy may be complete." (John 16:23–24)

This seems strange at first glance, but don't be put off. James wrote in his letter (James 4:2): *You do not have because you do not ask God.* It may seem that asking is just about *all* we do in some of our prayers. But there is something significant in the asking of a true disciple. He has come to the place of full dependence upon God for all he has and all he needs. The asking is done in that spirit—not for benefits and blessings, but for knowing and acknowledging God as provider of everything. A key is found in the phrase "in My name." That means according to who Jesus is—His character, His purposes, His grace and goodness. We are to ask what He would ask, with the commitment to use what God gives as Christ would use it—for the Father's glory and for His children's complete joy.

The apostle John, writing late in his life, reflects the same certainty that his Master had shown in that Upper Room, words that John had heard with his own ears: "Dear friends, if our hearts do not condemn us we have confidence before God, and can receive whatever we ask from Him because we keep His commands and do what is pleasing in His sight. Now this is His command: that we believe in the name of His Son Jesus Christ, and love one another as He commanded us. The one who keeps His commands remains in Him, and He in him. And the way we know that He remains in us is from the Spirit He has given us" (1 John 3:21–24). John was confident that what Jesus said is true. This promise has to do with much that Jesus said in John 14–16. We receive what we ask on two counts: (1) we obey God's commands and (2) we do what is pleasing in His sight. And the keeping of His commands has to do with our abiding in Him, in a union of the life that we share. Remember what we said earlier: the life in Christ and the life in us is the same. He has given us His life, manifested through the indwelling of His Spirit. Obedience and relationship—we seek both as we climb to the higher ground.

Later in 1 John, the apostle reiterates the final prayer promise of the Gospels, which reflects all that Jesus came to do: "Now this is the confidence we have before Him: whenever we ask anything according to His will, He hears us. And if we know that He hears whatever we ask, we know that we have what we have asked Him for" (1 John 5:14–15). This promise affirms all that we have learned about Him and from Him. It says that the key to our relationship with the Father lies in knowing and doing His will. Asking according to His will is a key on two levels: first, without a consideration of His will in our prayers, they may not even be heard. John says that we know that He hears when we ask *according to His will.* Otherwise, it seems, we cannot be sure that He hears. Just asking because we have a need, or to help a loved one or friend, may not get God's ear. But second is the positive aspect of the promise: when we *do* ask according to His will, we *are* heard. And if we are heard, the answer is sure. In the matter of our asking, as in all of our praying—and indeed in all of our Christian life—God's will must come first, before all personal desire and before all of our sympathies and compassions for the needs of others.

This makes it imperative, fellow traveler, that we look to the hill we climb in part 3 of this book as the place to learn to pray the Scriptures. Praying God's Word is the sure way to know that we are asking according to His will. His Word *is* His will.

Before we begin our time in part 3, however, we'll consider a final point, one that bears upon our attitude toward our prayers and how seriously we take our praying. Next we will discuss *intentionality* in our life of prayer.

REFLECTION

Date_____

To Consider: Take a moment to reflect on what you have learned about Jesus' prayer promises in this chapter.

Has there been an occasion in your life when you, or others, have been perplexed about these promises? Describe the situation.

_____

_____

_____

_____

Do you feel better prepared now to deal with such questions? What would be your response to such a question now? _____

_____

_____

_____

How do you think the lesson of this chapter might help you reach higher ground in your prayer life? _____

_____

_____

_____

How do you think your own prayers might change as a result of your study of Jesus' promises?_____

_____

_____

_____

Write a brief prayer for wisdom in applying in your own life
what you've learned in this chapter. _____

_____

_____

_____

_____

_____

You may want to add this prayer to your own.

Father, help me to see myself
in the same position as those disciples who heard the Master
give great and precious promises
for all who seek to follow Him to the higher ground
of deep and abiding fellowship with You.
Help me to understand that prayer is a matter of the heart,
and that if the desire of my heart is to bring glory to you,
to bear much fruit for You,
to do always what pleases You,
then my prayers will be answered in ways that will
accomplish all of those things.
You will be glorified, and my relationship with You
will be as You desire it to be.
I praise You and honor You,
asking these things in the name of
my gracious Lord Jesus Christ,
amen.

CHAPTER 9

Intentional Prayer

O ne vital principle we learn from our Lord is this: *we must be intentional in our prayer life.* We can't reach higher ground with casual prayer, and we can't cultivate a meaning-ful personal relationship with our Lord on a hit-or-miss basis. Faith, obedience, commitment—and now intentionality—all are necessary at the onset of the journey.

Move Beyond Casual Prayer

Many Christians, unready to grow in their prayer life, become content with small, casual, ineffective praying. Even at the ground level where our journey started, most of us were pretty inept at it. Sometimes even the experienced pray-ers among us were disappointed in the feebleness of our prayers.

Why was that true?

If we admit it, we must say that it was because we had not yet grasped the full significance and potential power of prayer in our lives and the lives of others. We wanted to do it, and sincerely did our best (so we reasoned), but we were dis-appointed and unsettled about it.

We may have studied prayer, attended conferences, heard sermons, and joined home prayer groups. But we were not con-vinced that what we said was what God heard.

A twentieth-century Norwegian teacher by the name of O. Hallesby wrote one of the classic books on prayer. The title is, simply and appropriately, *Prayer.*[1] In his book, Hallesby helps us understand that for most of us as we begin our journey, our idea of prayer is far short of God's idea of prayer. Hallesby is right.

Face it: most of us think of prayer as primarily asking God for things, for blessings, for healing, for safety, and so on. Now that kind of asking is not wrong; Jesus taught us to ask, and He gave some assurances that—under conditions we will learn about in chapter 13—we can expect positive answers.

But, says Prof. Hallesby, there are two things that form the attitude of the heart that God recognizes as prayer. One is faith, which we've seen as the first essential on our journey. The other is *helplessness.* Though we may not be enthusiastic about it, we know that he is right. The Bible is clear on this subject.

Do you consider yourself helpless? Most of us really don't. It's not the American way, is it? We're expected to be very self-sufficient, self-reliant, self-assured. To admit to helplessness is counter to what we've all been encouraged to believe. But for the Christian, it is necessary. Give an ear to the words of Jesus: "Apart from me you can do nothing" (John 15:5 NIV). This is His simple but comprehensive statement about our helplessness. It's where we are, regardless of our financial position or our technological prowess or our esteem in the eyes of men. Apart from Him, there is absolutely nothing we can do that is of any lasting value. In the context of His word picture—Himself as the vine and ourselves as the branches—He was giving a lesson of life: that is, true, eternal, God-given life.

Apart from Him, we cannot reach higher ground. We cannot know deeper truth. We can do nothing. But we are not apart from Him. We have Him! And with Him, everything is possible. You can find higher ground and know the deeper truth that God desires to reveal to you.

Begin by accepting your helplessness. Faith will be a continuing factor in all we say about this journey. Together, helplessness and faith enable prayer that God can recognize.

Plan for Your Prayer Time

Most of us make plans for just about everything else that we do, yet we still approach prayer with the idea that spontaneity is the greatest virtue. Whatever comes to mind is what we present to our heavenly Father. This is not all wrong, because it is basic to our relationship that we trust the Spirit within us to pray through us what is on the heart of God. And He will.

Still, this requires the intentionality to seek God's will in all that we do, all the time. If we are doing that, our connection with the Spirit is such that He has full access to our minds and hearts when we pray. But if not . . .

So here's a suggestion. Before you pray, pray. In the preliminary prayer time—maybe hours or maybe just moments before you come before the Father in intentional prayer—ask Him what you should pray about. It's amazing how quickly He will answer that prayer. Try it!

Once He has directed your prayer, spend time contemplating the circumstances or the needs of those for whom He has prompted you to pray. Consider Scriptures that relate to the specific needs or problems involved. Pray the appropriate Scriptures as you bring your petitions and intercessions to the throne of God. He is pleased when we pray His Word back to Him (this is the full thrust of part 3 of this book, just ahead).

Keep a Prayer Journal

A prayer journal is one of the best ways to develop and maintain intentionality. Write both names and needs—the specific desires of your own heart as well as those things that you know to be important in the lives of others. Here is the best place to look up and list Scripture verses (or even chapters) that best illustrate what you believe God may have on His mind concerning a certain person or issue. Voice the verse or verses, using your own name or the name of someone else in need. Write it down. And when God answers, be sure to write that down as well. Date it, and look back over your journal from time to time to be reminded of what God has done (read Deut. 8).

Pray Systematically

For many of us, our prayer lists can become unwieldy. We want to pray every day for those we know who have urgent needs, for our family, for our pastor and church, for our president, for missionaries, and the list goes on.

We have found it helpful to focus on praying for specific needs or specific groups on specific days. Our list is as follows:

Sunday: for our church and Bible fellowship class (We're aging, so there are many personal and family needs.)

Monday: for our family (children, grandchildren, extended family—though we pray for our children and grandchildren *every* day)

Tuesday: for our local, national, and world leaders

Wednesday: for those who are hurting (illness, broken families, job crisis)

Thursday: for the lost (primarily for family members who need Christ)

Friday: for others in ministry and for missions at all levels

Saturday: for ourselves, our health, our ministry

We pray every day, focusing on these groups as indicated, but also interceding for others with special needs that have come to our attention.

You can make your own list or organize your prayer in some other way. But this is intentional praying. It has focus and structure and consistency.

Expect Results

As you become more intentional in your praying, your prayer life will begin to change. Here are some of the things many of us have noticed quickly after setting our minds to becoming truly intentional:

- Our daily quiet time is no longer a matter of duty and habit, but of eager desire and deep concentration. We cease looking at the clock.
- Our prayer focus is no longer on ourselves, our needs, our personal advancement and welfare; now we pray for those things that Jesus, Paul, and Peter prayed for.
- We desire to pray as Jesus prayed—not only for the objects of His prayer but in His prayerful submission to the will of the Father.
- Our prayer life becomes disciplined conversation with the Father, through the Son, and in the power of the Holy Spirit.

Intentional Prayer in Bible Reading

One of the most important factors in intentional prayer is the Word itself, that is, praying as you read and as you study what God has revealed of Himself and His purposes.

So far in part 2, we've discussed the teaching and example of Jesus as preparation for effectiveness in our own prayer lives. This has been mostly about the *how* of praying.

As we begin chapter 10 and move into part 3, we focus on the *content* of our praying: the *what*. Our presentation of the *what* is not meant to be exclusive and limiting for you. You will pray as God directs you, and He will direct your praying in ways that are right for *you*, in keeping with His plans for you and for those for whom you pray.

In chapter 10 you'll find encouragement to pray *as you make your way through the Bible* in your normal quiet time, as well as in your more extended times of Bible study. You'll find an overview of different ways to pray as you go, along with sample prayers that will perhaps set a pattern for you to follow as you read and pray.

By the way, the prayers we write in this book are not intended as substitutes for your own spontaneous "from-the-heart" responses to God in His Word or however He may speak to you. Our prayers are not better than yours. We present them as illustrations of ways to express what is on your heart.

In part 3 our focus will be on an aspect of prayer that will add strength and certainty to *any kind* of prayer. The Bible assures us (see 1 John 5:13–14) that when we pray according to God's will, we receive what we ask. This is not mysterious or magical. It simply aligns our prayers with all we have learned of the prayer life and teaching of our Lord. He did—always and only—what the Father gave Him to do, what pleased the Father. Everything He did was with the Father's glory, concern, and will in mind. We can pray that way too.

Our journey to higher ground has led us to this point. Let's not miss what God has in store for us next.

REFLECTION

Date_____

To Consider: Think over your prayers of the past few days or weeks.

Have you spent more of your prayer time talking, rather than listening? If so, why do you think that's true? (If not, congratulations; you're in the minority!)_____

_____

_____

_____

_____

What is your biggest hurdle to listening? (Not enough time, habit, lack of focus, distractions?)_____

_____

_____

_____

_____

In what way do you think your prayer life might become stronger if you developed a listening ear and began to talk with— rather than *to*—God when you pray?_____

_____

_____

_____

_____

Pause to write a prayer for God's help in this area of your prayer life._____

_____

_____

_____

_____

_____

_____

You may want to add this prayer to your own.

> *Father, You are a great and awesome God,*
> *and I'm amazed that You want to converse with me—*
> *You are not the author of confusion,*
> *but the God of peace.*
> *Grant me listening ears,*
> *that I may hear Your still, quiet voice;*
> *help me to listen with my heart,*
> *to set my mind on You and on the things of the Spirit.*
> *Good Shepherd,*
> *help me to hear and recognize Your voice,*
> *in Jesus' name, amen.*

CHAPTER 10

Praying Your Way through God's Word

By way of preparation for your journey into the practice of praying God's Word in part 3, we present suggested approaches to praying specific parts of Scripture as you encounter them in your normal approach to Bible reading. This will help as you go deeper into Scripture praying in part 3.

Because we are convinced that your daily quiet time, alone with God, is the heart, the center, of your prayer life (representing, as it does, your first meeting with Him every day), we begin with some suggestions that will encourage you to connect the two significant elements—the quiet time and praying the Word. You will have other periods of Bible reading and study, so the same principles and recommendations will apply at any time of day. But why not begin with your quiet time, and see what God might do to make His Word come alive in those private moments with Him?

Cultivate the Habit of Praying as You Read

Open your Bible with a simple prayer, asking not only for enlightenment and understanding of the meaning of what you read, but also to see how it applies to your life. Anticipate a word from God: encouragement, love, guidance, wisdom, sometimes correction. As you begin, affirm that your heart's desire is to obey—in His strength—anything He asks you to do (James 1:22).

We recommend following a plan that takes you through the entire Bible in an organized fashion so that the Spirit has the freedom to speak from chapters many of us would rather avoid because they are difficult to understand or, frankly, are not pleasant reading. It's all God's Word, and it's all important for us to be exposed to. Of course, you don't have to read the Bible this way, but we hope you will, at least to the extent that you will have read through the entire Bible several times over a lifetime.

Whatever your plan, it is important to read the Word with the intent of application and communion with God. This means not reading simply to keep on track and check off chapters each day, but coming with your heart prepared to meet with God personally. Even when you follow a plan that keeps you accountable to move through the Scriptures in an orderly way, your time in the Word should not be rushed. You may have only fifteen minutes. If you only cover one verse, yet you have the sense of God speaking to you, that's more than sufficient.

Read, Pause, Listen, and Pray

The general process of Bible reading consists of these four steps: read, pause, listen, and pray. You've opened your Bible with a prayer, and now you begin to read with the thought in mind that God has given you His Word to help you understand Him and His purposes. After you read a verse, a thought, a sentence, or a passage, pause to think about what you've read and how it might apply to your life. Give the Spirit the opportunity to show you something about the verse. If nothing particular seems meant for you personally, keep on reading thoughtfully. If the Spirit stops at a point and does give you an impression of significance for your life in some way, mark the verse. You may want to put a date beside it, with a brief note, or write a reference to it in your journal in order to record more thoughts than the margin of your Bible will hold.

You won't likely hear a direct word from God every time you read, but it's a good idea to note it when you do.

The following examples demonstrate how this might work with different parts of Scripture. Some passages lend themselves more readily to this than others.

- "Be glad for all God is planning for you. Be patient in trouble, and always be prayerful" (Rom. 12:12 NLT).

   Father, I know that You know what's best, and that Your plans are always best for me. But I'm facing a rough time right now, and I need Your strength. Help me to remember to pray my way through, and to see what You have in mind for my next steps.

- "Whatever you ask in My name, I will do it so that the Father may be glorified in the Son" (John 14:13).

   Lord, I understand Your promise. Help me to know how to pray so that what I ask will bring glory to the Father, and that Your name will be lifted up.

Parables

When reading the parables, read through and then reflect on what you've read. What point was Jesus making? Then apply it to your life, if you can see a way to do that, and present what you see to God. Here are some examples:

- Parable of the Sower (Matt. 13:3–9)

    Father, I want my heart to be good soil, where the seed of Your Word, Your truth, can be nourished and grow. Help me to guard my heart and keep it pure before You.
- Parable of the Good Samaritan (Luke 10:30–36)

    Lord, I've known the truth of this parable for many years—and yet I find myself failing to be what You would want me to be for those in need. Help me to see people as You see them, and help me to see every opportunity to help as an opportunity to show them Your love.

History, People, and Events

As you would with any story you read, try to imagine the scene and setting as it must have happened. Think of yourself as one of the characters. How would you feel if you were one of the individuals in the passages below?

- "Saul answered Samuel, 'I have sinned. I have transgressed the Lord's command and your words. Because I was afraid of the people, I obeyed them. Now therefore, please forgive my sin and return with me so I can worship the Lord.' Samuel replied to Saul, 'I will not return with you. Because you rejected the word of the Lord, the Lord has rejected you from being king over Israel'" (1 Sam. 15:24–27).

    Father, help me not to be afraid of the people as Saul was—not to care so much about what others think of me. Keep me strong so I won't ever deliberately disobey You!
- "Daniel determined that he would not defile himself with the king's food or with the wine he drank. So he asked permission from the chief official not to defile himself. God had granted Daniel favor and compassion

from the chief official. . . . At the end of 10 days they [Daniel, Shadrach, Meshach, and Abednego] looked better and healthier than all the young men who were eating the king's food. So the guard continued to remove their food and the wine they were to drink and gave them vegetables" (Dan. 1:8–9, 15–16).

Lord, I so admire Daniel. I want to be like him in character, to have the courage to stand firm, especially if I'm expected to go along with something that is clearly not Your will. Give me the courage.

Psalms

Many of the psalms are prayers, and that makes them especially easy and appropriate to pray. Even if we can't directly relate to some of the verses, they can give us cause for thanksgiving or praise. Consider the following example:

- "All who hate me whisper together about me; they plan to harm me" (Ps. 41:7).

   Father, reading what David wrote makes me so grateful for the life You have given me. I don't think I have any enemies whispering about me or planning to harm me, unless it's evil spirits. If so, I know that I'm safe and secure in You, my shelter and my stronghold.

There are many verses of worship and praise, many promises found in the Psalms that will find their way into our prayers as we grow increasingly familiar with them. For example:

- "Take delight in the Lord, and He will give you your heart's desires" (Ps. 37:4).

   Father, my great desire is to take delight in You, not for Your blessings and benefits, but because I know and love You. Help me to know You better and love You more every day of my life. Put Your desires in my heart, that I may want only what You want for me and those I love.

- "For the Lord God is a sun and shield. The Lord gives grace and glory; He does not withhold the good from those who live with integrity" (Ps. 84:11).

  Lord, I love the image of You as a sun and shield. You bring light into my life on the darkest days. You protect me even when I don't know I need it. You give me grace that sustains me and the glory of knowing You. Thank You for Your promise not to withhold good from those who live with integrity. That's how I want to live—so that what I believe and stand for is played out in my life. Help me to live that way, for I know it will be pleasing to You.

Proverbs

The proverbs lend themselves readily to prayer.

- "The name of the Lord is a strong tower; the righteous run to it and are protected" (Prov. 18:10).

  Father, I can see how Your name is a strong tower because Your name represents You, and You are our strength, all we'll need to face anything in life. I thank You that I may run to You in the righteousness of Christ. Help me to live a righteous life—according to Your will—as best I'm able. Forgive me when I fail.

- "Let another praise you, and not your own mouth— a stranger, and not your own lips" (Prov. 27:2).

  Lord, help me never to call attention to myself or my own accomplishments. I know that whatever good I may do is a gift from You, and I have no reason to boast. Help me to give You the praise and to practice humility in my life, today and every day.

In closing this chapter and in preparation for the instruction to come in part 3, let us again say: the point of reading the Bible in this way is to help us read not merely for information but for application, growth, and, most of all, as our primary means of receiving a personal word from our God.

REFLECTION

Date:_____

To Consider: think of the time you have spent reading the Bible over the past months and years, as well as more recently.

Are you typically reading the Bible on a daily basis? If yes, why has that been important to you? If not, why not? What is your biggest hurdle to consistency?_____

_____

_____

_____

_____

Have you typically considered reading the Bible as an important discipline because it is God's Word and you know you should be familiar with it? Or have you approached it as a time to meet with God personally? In what ways have either—or both—been important to you?_____

_____

_____

_____

_____

What is the one thing you feel in need of when you consider reading the Bible daily?_____

_____

_____

_____

Why do you think what you've written is important to you?

_____

_____

_____

_____

Take a moment to write a brief prayer asking God's help to make your Bible reading more consistent or meaningful than it is now, no matter how significant it presently is:_____

_____

_____

_____

_____

_____

You may want to add this prayer to your own.

Father, I want the Bible to become
more alive to me than it's ever been,
to be more living and active in my life than I've ever known it to be.
I want it to be the lamp to my feet and the light to my path

that I know it is meant to be.
May I never approach it as just another book.
I want the time that I spend reading the Bible to be time with You.
I want to sense Your presence and hear Your voice,
to pick the Bible up praying, speaking to You,
and anticipating Your answer.
Help that time with You and Your Word
become increasingly more important and meaningful to me,
for I ask in Jesus' name—the Word of God—amen.

Part 3

Praying God's Word

AT THIS POINT IN YOUR journey, our hope and prayer is that you will have spent some significant moments in prayer and reflection over the principles of prayer that Jesus taught. We all need to understand and practice them until they become daily habits of prayer, as natural as breathing.

We can never get away from these principles if we want to keep our relationship with God on track for higher ground. Prayer that has God's Word at the very heart of it moves us closer to Him. We strongly believe that learning to pray God's Word will be the greatest single advancement for your prayer life. Continuing to pray as you've been taught here, day in and day out, will keep you on higher ground.

To encourage you to make Scripture praying a cornerstone of your prayer life, we devote this section of *Higher Ground, Deeper Truth* to practical examples of how to pray Scripture in a variety of ways, to enrich every kind of prayer. We know the Lord will be pleased, and we pray that you and those you pray for will be richly blessed.

There Is Power in the Word—and in Praying the Word

The Word of God is living and active, filled with the *dunamis* power of the Holy Spirit. *Dunamis* is the Greek word that is often used to describe the Holy Spirit's power; it's the word from which we derive *dynamite* and *dynamic*. It's the power that changes hearts and lives as we read—or pray—the Scripture.

- "For the word of God is living and active. Sharper than any double-edged sword, it penetrates even to dividing soul and spirit, joints and marrow; it judges the thoughts and attitudes of the heart" (Heb. 4:12 NIV).
- "[S]o is my word that goes out from my mouth: *It will not return to me empty, but will accomplish what I desire and achieve the purpose for which I sent it*" (Isa. 55:11 NIV, emphasis added).
- "Is not my word like fire," declares the LORD, "and like a hammer that breaks a rock in pieces?" (Jer. 23:29 NIV).
- "Your word is a lamp for my feet and a light on my path" (Ps. 119:105).

These verses are an encouragement to our hearts that prayers filled with God's Word will release the power of His will to accomplish His purpose, to break the rocks of strongholds and hardened hearts, to provide guidance and direction that will keep us and others on His path.

Consider this as well: Scripture is not only infused with the power of the Spirit, but also with the life and power of our Savior.

- "In the beginning was the Word, and the Word was with God, and the Word was God. . . . Through him all things were made; without him nothing was made that has been made. In him was life" (John 1:1, 3a NIV).
- "[H]is [Jesus'] name is the Word of God" (Rev. 19:13 NIV).
- "I write to you, young men, because you are strong, and *the word of God lives in you*" (1 John 2:14b NIV, emphasis added).

Jesus is identified as the Word of God, the One who embodies the creative power of God, the One through whom all things were made. The Word, which is living and active, which lives in us, is the very essence of Christ, who is able to use it—as we pray it for ourselves and others—to change us at the very core of our being. We pray about people, issues, and concerns, and when we include Scripture in our prayers, these words of prayer from God's Word will be an expression of our heart and His will—and they will in some way release God's presence and power in answer to our prayer. Consider this in light of a verse we've already noted: "Now this is the confidence we have before Him: *whenever we ask anything according to His will,* He hears us. And if we know that He hears whatever we ask, we know that *we have what we have asked* Him for" (1 John 5:14–15, emphasis added). Praying God's Word is praying His will.

Taking a Stand in Prayer

As we pray the Word, we are taking a stand in prayer, strong in the Lord and in His mighty power: "Finally, be strong in the Lord and in his mighty power. . . . Put on the full armor of God, so that when the day of evil comes, you may be able to stand your ground. . . . Stand firm . . . take . . . the sword of the Spirit, which is the word of God. And pray in the Spirit on all occasions with all kinds of prayers and requests. With this in mind, be alert and always keep on praying for all the saints" (Eph. 6:10, 13, 14a, 17b–18 NIV).

Our emphasis here is on taking a stand in prayer. (We'll have more to say about the armor of God in a later chapter.) When Paul refers to the sword of the Spirit as the word of God, he uses the Greek word *rhema,* which refers to the spoken word—the Word spoken in prayer. He says we are to use it as we pray in the Spirit—led by the Spirit, empowered by the Spirit—who will hand us the right sword, at the right time, for the right person. The Bible is not so much our sword as it is our arsenal of weapons. Every word, verse, precept, or principle becomes a weapon in prayer, whether we're standing against the powers of darkness or simply praying as Paul says we must—on all occasions with all kinds of prayers and requests.

Christians who read and study the Word with hearts that are right and open to the work of the Spirit begin to be infused with the Word. It becomes part of us, and because it is living and creative—and filled with the will, the truths, and the purposes of God—it cannot help becoming part of our prayers. Listen to the prayers of mature Christians. They will not be quoting chapter and verse, but their prayers will be filled with the Word and ignited by the power of the Spirit. The Spirit and the Truth just come forth!

Directing Our Minds in Prayer

When we pray the Word of God, we are praying with our spirit as led and directed by the Spirit, but Paul said he also prayed with his mind (1 Cor. 14:15). We have that responsibility as well. Certainly one way we can do that, with an eye to praying the Scriptures, is that we must prepare our minds by filling them with God's Word. Then as we pray, we use our minds to focus our thoughts and prayers as the Spirit leads. This will be the heart of our discussion about praying God's Word—we must begin every prayer with a deliberate directing of our mind toward God and the things of God.

We will be discussing many types of prayer in this section—worship, surrender, confession, supplication—and in each case we will be providing examples of how our prayers may be strengthened by adding appropriate Scriptures to them. We will encourage and reinforce the necessity of pausing before we pray to focus on God—who He is, what He is like, and how He works in our lives.

We'll be illustrating how to focus our hearts and minds toward a different part of God's nature and character, as revealed by His names and attributes, in a way that is pertinent to our specific prayers. We'll move from the general to the specific in every aspect of prayer through Scriptures. This is simple and easy to do if we will allow ourselves to discipline our minds. If we are consistent, praying with Scripture will soon become an ingrained habit that will elevate our praying to a new level and draw us closer to God.

Now let's illustrate what we've just said.

CHAPTER 11

Affirming the Relationship through God's Word

The framework for our discussion of adding Scripture to our prayers will be the principles of prayer that Jesus taught. They are the foundation for our relationship with God; we must never depart from them, but rather continue to expand our understanding and application of what they are about. This is a lifelong process, and we want to help you—and ourselves—find ways of extending these principles and making them more meaningful by adding Scripture to our daily prayers in an intentional, purposeful way.

Keep in mind, too, that you will not be able to incorporate these suggestions all at once—that would be overwhelming. The Spirit will show you where to begin, based upon where you are in your prayer life. We encourage you to see praying God's Word not as a once-and-for-all project, but as ongoing growth in prayer, one step at a time as you go.

We begin, then, where Jesus began, with "Our Father in heaven," focusing our attention on our eternal relationship with God. We come humbly, knowing He is Almighty God, yet blessed that we are able to come as dependent children— respectful, yet eager for His company. As we come, we pause to first turn our minds to focus on our Father, not ourselves, not our needs, not the needs of others.

We begin our daily prayers by affirming this relationship. We can simply say "Our Father," but He is so much more. We often have a nebulous idea of God, thinking of Him more as a concept than the very real person that He is. The whole Bible tells about Him, presenting hundreds of names, attributes, and descriptions that affirm and extend our knowledge of who He is. (When we refer to the "names of God," we are speaking generically to include names, titles, and descriptions of God the Father, Jesus the Son, and the Holy Spirit.)

Using these names and attributes is not only honoring to God, but it gives us a greater understanding of who He is and in what ways He is willing to relate personally to us. It helps focus the direction of our prayers and makes them more intentional. God's nature is like a multifaceted diamond—each of His names is like a different facet, revealing a different part of His nature.

Names and Attributes of Our Father

As we come into God's presence and consider our Father, we pause to think of Him in that role. This should be a time of rejoicing in our hearts that He is our Father, a time of affirmation as to what that means, and a few Scriptures (verses, names, or attributes) will come to mind. As you pray day to day, different Scriptures will likely come to you, depending on what's going on in your life, what's on your heart for prayer. This is a dynamic process, led by the Spirit.

As we focus here on God our Father, let's use the questions

we mentioned in the introduction and see what descriptions of God our Father the Spirit might typically bring to mind. (You will find this list repeated in the appendix with Scripture references.)

Who God Is

Father
Creator
Maker
Potter
Abba Father

What He Is Like

Love unfailing
Merciful
Gracious
Gentle

How He Works in Our Lives

His hands formed me.
His hands knit me together.
His hands spin me on His potter's wheel.
He sent His Son to die for me.
He has made me His masterpiece.
He has written my name in His book of life.
He created me for good works He has planned.
He has a plan and purpose for my life.
He will fulfill His purpose for me.
He is making me like Christ.
He guards me as the apple of His eye.
He considers me precious and valued in His sight.
He rejoices over me with singing.

Do you see how pausing to direct your thoughts of God toward a certain facet of His nature helps bring illuminating Scriptures to mind? Such Scriptures magnify Him as our Father; they make Him larger in our sight. When we magnify Him, it's as though that facet of His person and nature is revealed more clearly. Somehow it helps bring Him into sharper focus in our mind's eye.

Reading and Learning the Word

Obviously, the more familiar we are with the Bible, the more we will begin to remember Scripture truths like these. We may not remember where to find them in the Bible, at least not at first, but if we begin to use them in our prayers, write them in our journal, maybe even make an effort to memorize them, they will naturally become part of our prayers. They are in our hearts and minds, released as we pray.

You'll find that the more intentional, the more focused and prepared you become about affirming the relationship (or any of the other principles of prayer that we'll be discussing), the more you will begin to organize them in your mind. It may help if you start a journal and begin to keep your own lists so you can remember verses you want to include in your prayers.

Let's take a look at how this intentional focus translates into prayer.

Sample Prayers for Affirming the Relationship
(These prayers are reprinted in the appendix.)

Father,

Thank You for giving me life, for being my Creator and my Maker. Thank You for sending Jesus to die for me. It's wonderful that because He did, no one can snatch me out of Your hand!

*I'm grateful that You have a plan and purpose for my life and
that You will fulfill it, that it's not all my responsibility.*

*Abba, Father, thank You for Your unfailing love, for protect-
ing me as the apple of Your eye. I'm so very grateful to belong to
You!*

This brief prayer incorporates truths from ten of the
Scriptures we listed; it takes about half a minute to pray. We
didn't use all of the Scriptures we mentioned above, but you
could. You also could move prayerfully through the whole list,
as we've done in the following prayer. (Note that both the list of
Scriptures and the following prayer are included in the appendix.) This longer prayer takes only a couple of minutes to pray.

Father,

*It's a joy to come as Your child, knowing You are my Creator
and my Maker. Your hands formed me, knit me together in my
mother's womb, and even today, they're spinning me on Your
Potter's wheel.*

*Thank You for loving me so much that You sent Your only Son
to die for me. Thank You for Your promise that no one can snatch
me out of Your hand; I'm secure in Your grip. It's wonderful to
think that You have engraved my name on the palms of Your
hands and written it in Your book of life!*

*It thrills me to know that You see me as Your masterpiece—
even though I can't always see it. You have created me for the good
works that You have prepared for me to do. I know that even
when I don't realize it, You have a plan and purpose for my life.
You will fulfill Your purpose for me, no matter how many mistakes I may make along the way. There is comfort in that and in
knowing that You are making me like Christ.*

*Father, You are full of unfailing love, and mercy, and grace—
my gentle, tender, Abba Father, You are very dear to me.*

*You protect me as the apple of Your eye. You see me as precious
and valued in Your sight. You rejoice over me with singing—what
a marvelous thought!*

I'm so very grateful to belong to You!

Such prayers are not only pleasing to God as they affirm
the truth of His Word, but they are affirming to us as we pray
them. Every time we pray such Scriptures of affirmation, they
become lodged more securely in our minds and hearts, and the
Spirit is able to bring them to mind at times when we may
feel discouraged or defeated, reminding us who we are as God's
children—who we are in Christ.

Do you see how such praying might be helpful to those who
have trouble relating to God as Father? There are some who will
say they can't relate to God as Father because they didn't have a
father at home in their childhood or teenage years, or because
their father was distant, totally authoritarian, never expressed
his love for them, or was even abusive. When we fill our minds
and hearts with affirming Scriptures, however, the living Word
opens our hearts to receive His love in a new way.

It Doesn't Take Long

One more thought before moving on: Don't be overwhelmed
by the idea of this process. It takes longer to write about it than
it actually takes to follow through in prayer. It happens naturally
as we pray with our minds set to focus in a certain direction. Ask
the Spirit to direct your thoughts and bring Scripture to mind,
and then trust Him to do it. Ultimately, you won't even have to
think about it; you will pray in a direction, and the Scriptures

will spring into your mind. Let this become a habit—using Scriptures to help you pray your way to higher ground.

REFLECTION

Date:_____

To Consider: think of the chapter you have just read.

What is the one thing that stands out that you might want to incorporate (for the first time or in increasing measure) into your personal prayers? _____

_____

_____

_____

_____

Why do you think this might be important for you? _____

_____

_____

_____

_____

What is the first step you might take?_____

_____

_____

_____

_____

Write a brief prayer, asking for God's help. _____

_____

_____

_____

_____

_____

You may want to add this prayer to your own.

> *Father, show me better and more complete ways*
> *to express my heart to You in prayer.*
> *Help me to slow down my prayers,*
> *not to rush into Your presence, not to hurry through.*
> *May my prayers be like a sweet-smelling incense to You,*
> *and give You pleasure.*
> *In Jesus' name, amen.*

CHAPTER 12

Enhancing Our Worship through God's Word

As we approach ways to enrich our personal worship, keep in mind the simple idea of focusing heart and mind on God by pausing briefly to reflect on: who God is, what He is like, and how He works in our lives. We'll continue to refer to and incorporate this principle as we move through the next chapters.

Hallowing God's Name

There is a reason why Jesus specifically said we should "hallow God's name" rather than simply saying we should "worship God." To fully appreciate this, we must keep in mind that in biblical times, a person's name represented his character. We've already mentioned that there are hundreds of names, titles, and descriptions of God in the Bible, and each one represents a facet of His nature.

Using His names personalizes our worship, our prayers, and our relationship with Him. Using a particular name says, in essence, "I know who You are, what You're like, how You work in the world." Using His names is honoring to Him because it shows that we have invested the time to learn the names, have sought to understand how they describe Him, and have disciplined our minds to use them. Aren't we pleased when someone remembers and uses our names?

But of course, there is more to it than pleasing God. Just as the Scriptures of affirmation in the last chapter help us comprehend God as our Father and establish our identity as His children, so bringing Scriptures with His various names and attributes into our worship helps enlarge our view of God. As we hallow His name, such worship embeds the reality of who He is into the consciousness of our hearts and minds.

Using God's names in worship as we begin our daily prayers helps remind us that He is truly sufficient for any need or concern. It helps turn our minds away from even the most overwhelming needs we're praying about and direct them toward the One who can help. It's one of the ways we keep our eyes on Him (Heb. 12:2a; Ps. 141:8a), and it builds our faith. God doesn't want our worship to build His own pride or ego. He doesn't need our worship (though He is pleased with it), but He knows how much *we* need such worship and how much it will ultimately mean to us.

God Seeks Worshippers

God seeks those who will worship Him in spirit and in truth: "Yet a time is coming and has now come when the true worshipers will worship the Father *in spirit and truth,* for they are the kind of *worshipers the Father seeks*" (John 4:23 NIV, emphasis added). If this describes the worshippers God is seeking, and if we want to please Him, we must be among those who worship Him in spirit and in truth. We worship Him in spirit from our innermost heart, where our spirit has been made alive with the Spirit of God. This is worship from a true sense of awe at being in the presence of a holy God. It says we are coming reverently into His presence, pausing to quiet ourselves and turns our minds and hearts toward the One we serve. Our prayer to affirm our relationship to Him, child to Father, is part of this preparation.

We also must worship in truth—in the truth of who He is and the truth of who we are before Him. This puts our relationship with Him in perspective: He is God; we are not. He is our Creator; we are His creation. He is Teacher; we are students. He is King; we are servants. He is Commander; we are soldiers. Worshipping in truth is worshipping Him in respect of His authority and in the full realization of His character: He is not only our God of love, mercy, kindness, and grace, but He is also holy, righteous, and just. Worshipping in truth is worship according to the truth of what the Bible says about Him—in the truth of who He is, not our personal impression of Him or who we want Him to be. We are not to worship the God of our favorite verses, but God as He is revealed through all of His Word. Worshipping Him by His names and attributes is one of the best ways to do that.

We Worship by the Spirit of God

It's comforting to know that the Spirit of God will help us worship in spirit and in truth: "For it's not where we worship that counts, but how we worship—is our worship spiritual and real? Do we have the Holy Spirit's help? *For God is Spirit, and we must have his help to worship as we should.* The Father wants this kind of worship from us" (John 4:23–24 TLB, emphasis added). The apostle Paul also tells us: "For it is we who are the circumcision, we who worship *by the Spirit of God*" (Phil. 3:3b NIV, emphasis added).

So, how does the Spirit enable our worship? Certainly the Spirit brings Scriptures to mind. But more than that, He helps us to know God better and experience more of the love of Christ: "I keep asking that the God of our Lord Jesus Christ, the glorious Father, *may give you the Spirit of wisdom and revelation, so that you may know him better. I pray also that the eyes of your heart may be enlightened.* . . . I pray that out of his glorious riches he may *strengthen you with power through his Spirit in your inner being, so that Christ may dwell in your hearts through faith* . . . [and that you may] *grasp how wide and long and high and deep is the love of Christ*" (Eph. 1:17–18a; 3:16–18 NIV, emphasis added). It is God's Spirit who enlightens the eyes of our hearts to know Him and His love. If we are in tune with such enlightenment, can our response be anything but worship, praise, and adoration?

The Spirit encourages our worship by bringing God's names and attributes to mind, but first we must put them there for the Spirit to draw from. As we read the Bible, we will naturally absorb some of God's names and attributes; but many find it helpful and even thrilling to begin collecting lists of God's names and intentionally learning them.

Worship Is an Attitude of the Heart

Our worship involves more than an expression of prayer and the words we use; it's an attitude of the heart as well: "Therefore, I urge you, brothers, in view of God's mercy, *to offer your bodies as living sacrifices,* holy and pleasing to God—*this is your spiritual act of worship*" (Rom. 12:1 NIV, emphasis added). Surrendering ourselves is, in itself, a spiritual act of worship. We'll talk more about surrender in the next chapter and suggest ways to deepen and intensify our surrender of self to God as well as give appropriate Scriptures for prayer. But for now, it's important to realize that it doesn't matter how many names of God we learn and use if our hearts, motives, and actions are not surrendered to Him in the process. If we desire to worship by the Spirit of God—and if we must have His help to do it in spirit and in truth—our surrender is not an option. It is essential to our worship. The Spirit is quenched when we are full of self.

Lifting the Banner

In worship, one way of focusing our thoughts toward a specific name of God is to think of it as lifting a banner (today we would call it a "flag") that carries His name—a banner to stand beneath, proclaiming our allegiance and service to our God whose name we raise. In biblical times armies raised banners as they encamped beneath them, and they carried banners before them as they advanced. It is still true today: platoons, companies, brigades, regiments—all have their flags.

The idea of placing God's name on a banner isn't ours; it's His. God identified Himself by one of His *Jehovah* names after He helped Joshua defeat the Amalekites. At that time Moses was on the hill holding up his staff as the armies fought. When his staff was raised, Joshua's army won; when his arms grew tired and he dropped them, they lost. Finally, Aaron and Hur came alongside Moses to support his arms and the battle was won. After the victory, Moses built an altar to *Jehovah-Nissi*, meaning "the LORD is my banner" (Exod. 17:15).

Isaiah also affirmed the Lord as our banner when he declared that one day Jesus (the Root of Jesse) would stand as our banner (Isa. 11:10a NIV).

So as we come to worship, we lift our banner, selecting different names of God to raise in worship. We do this by asking the Spirit of God to help us express our love and adoration, our awesome respect for who God is as our Shepherd (or Protector, Provider, Healer, etc.). The more familiar we become with God's names—with verses, words, and phrases of worship—the more the Spirit will be able to enlarge our view of God and help us enrich our worship in ways that are pleasing to Him.

Note in our examples of prayer that we are using familiar biblical words of worship: *worship, adore, exalt, extol, magnify, revere.* These are not words that are part of our everyday conversation, and for most of us they seem formal and stilted. We hope that won't stop you from trying them out in your private prayer times, because they give you gracious ways to express your heart toward God. If you'll practice using them, they'll soon seem natural.

Now, let's come to worship, this time focusing our minds on God as our Protector. We lift His name on our banner and set our mind's eye in that direction. (You will find the following lists of God's names and attributes in the appendix with the verse references.)

Lifting the Banner: Protector

Who He Is

Protector
Defender
Mighty Warrior
Commander of the army of the Lord
Strong and mighty God
Wall of fire

What He Is Like

Ever-present help in trouble
Almighty
Faithful
Trustworthy

How He Works in Our Lives

Keeps us
Watches over us
Guards us from behind
Goes before us
Shelters us beneath His wings
Holds us with His victorious right hand

Sample Prayer for Worshipping Our Protector

(This prayer is reprinted in the appendix.)

Father,

I come to worship You, lifting high Your name as my Protector. I exalt You as my Defender, my mighty Warrior, the Commander of the army of heaven, strong and mighty God, my ever-present help in times of danger. I rejoice in Your faithfulness, knowing You are my keeper who watches over me. You are trustworthy, and I can count on You to go before me and to guard me from behind.

I magnify Your name as the wall of fire around me, as the One who shelters me beneath Your wings, who holds me by Your victorious right hand. With You as my protector, I have no reason to be fearful or afraid!

Lifting the banner brings God our Protector into focus. The more often we pray this way, the more real any given side of

God's nature and character becomes and the more readily specific names and attributes will spring to life in extemporaneous prayer when we need them.

REFLECTION

Date:_____

To Consider: Think of the chapter you have just read.

What is the one thing that stands out that you might want to incorporate (for the first time or in increasing measure) into your personal prayers? _____

_____

_____

_____

_____

Why do you think this might be important for you? _____

_____

_____

_____

_____

What is the first step you might take?_____

_____

_____

_____

_____

Write a brief prayer, asking for God's help. _____

_____

_____

_____

_____

_____

_____

You may want to add this prayer to your own.

Father help me to learn more about You—
who You are, what You are like,
and how You work in our lives—every day.
Help me to learn more about worshipping You,
about setting my mind on You as I begin to pray.
Expand my time of personal worship,
not only as I begin my day in prayer,
but as I continue through the day,
fill my mind with praises to You,
my Lord and my God.
In Jesus' name, amen.

CHAPTER 13

Growing in Surrender through God's Word

In our last chapter we said that surrender is essential to our worship. It is equally essential if we are to continue the pathway to higher ground in our relationship with the Lord.

God doesn't want just a part of our heart or our mind or our time. He wants everything. Absolute surrender is our only worthy posture in approaching Him in prayer. We must all keep in mind that words are no substitute for attitude. God knows our hearts, and it's not enough to say that we submit and give Him all. We must mean what we say. In our prayers—and from our hearts—it is important to show Him that we know Him as Master, Lord, and King.

Living Sacrifice: Surrender of Self

In the last chapter we looked at the following verse from Romans 12 as we emphasized our sacrifice of self as a spiritual act of worship. In this chapter we want to consider two other aspects of this verse: "Therefore, I urge you, brothers, *in view of God's mercy,* to offer your bodies as living sacrifices, holy and pleasing to God—this is your spiritual act of worship" (Rom. 12:1 NIV, emphasis added).

For most of us, surrender of self is a process. As we begin our Christian walk, we don't fully understand the implications of a complete surrender in our lives. We may not even be sure what we're supposed to be surrendering. But as we grow in our understanding of the Word and what it tells us of the life we're to live, we'll learn. As we move into the higher ground of personal relationship with God, we begin to understand that when Jesus says that unless we give up everything, we cannot be His disciples (Luke 14:33), He means it. He may not take everything, but we must let go so that He can if He chooses. The hardest thing to surrender may be self. It's not the idea of a general surrender ("I surrender all") but the specifics of intentional personal surrender that are most difficult.

We're not talking here about the broader issues of giving up everything in view of a call to Romania. We're talking about the more personal, sometimes little, things that can get in the way of moving to higher ground. For instance, most of us realize that if we want to have the sense of God speaking to us on a reasonably frequent basis, we can't rush through our quiet time. Yet if we want to expand our daily prayer life by incorporating more and different types of prayer (such as worship) by learning to pray with Scriptures, by reading the Bible prayerfully and pausing for prayer as we read—all that is going to take time. It doesn't have to be significantly more time—we don't have to add an hour to our quiet time immediately—but we must be willing to start somewhere, maybe with an extra ten to fifteen minutes.

For most of us that means we must give up something else to make room for more time with God. We may need to sacrifice our desire to sleep until the last possible moment in the morning. We may have to give up leisure reading or the late evening TV news. This type of sacrifice doesn't sound nearly as important as a sacrifice of lifestyle necessary to move onto the mission field, and in a way it may not be. But on the other hand, we're talking about the higher ground of *koinonia* fellowship with God. It would be possible for us to take our tendency toward busyness onto a mission field. We could serve twenty years in Africa or Asia without an in-depth personal relationship with God because we were more willing to make the large sacrifices than the less visible, but equally significant, ones.

Scripture Prayers Enable Deeper Levels of Surrender

In prayer, we should always take moments to pause and gather our thoughts, focusing our minds on what we're about—in this case, surrender.

1. First we pause and prayerfully reflect on who—and Whose—we are and why.

- I'm not my own, I belong to Christ, who bought me with His life (1 Cor. 6:19–20).
- I've been crucified with Christ (Gal. 2:20).
- I am His servant (Eph. 6:21).
- I'm a branch grafted into the Vine (John 15:5).

2. As we do, these verses become our brief prayer.
   Father,
       I acknowledge the truth that I am not my own, that
   I belong to Christ, who bought me with His life. I come

before You as His servant, a bond slave of Christ to sub-mit and surrender my life to You. As best I know my own heart, I hold nothing back.

3. Then we ask for God's help in our quest to become more wholly surrendered.

To reach the deeper levels of surrender, we become more specific, more intentional in our prayers. We call on Scripture to help us understand not only what we should be surrendering but what we should be asking for in our desire to be more like Christ. Surrender is not simply about giving up self, but about His life becoming more evident in us (John 3:30).

- Father, I give You my body; help me to offer myself as an instrument of righteousness (Rom. 6:13).
- I give You my mind; help me to have the mind of Christ (1 Cor. 2:16b).
- I give You my heart; help me to love You with all my heart, all my mind, all my strength (Matt. 22:37).
- I surrender my will to Your will; help me to deny myself and follow Christ (Luke 9:23).

Put Off the Old and Put On the New

Paul tells us that as new creations in Christ, the old (spiritual condition) is gone and the new (life in Christ) has come: "Therefore if anyone is in Christ, there is a new creation; old things have passed away, and look, new things have come" (2 Cor. 5:17). He also says we have a responsibility to put off the old and put on the new—the new attitude of our minds: "You were taught, with regard to your former way of life, to put off your old self, which is being corrupted by its deceitful desires; to be made new in the attitude of your minds; and to

put on the new self, created to be like God in true righteousness and holiness" (Eph. 4:22–24 NIV). That means change. We
should see new life in ourselves, a new ability to deal with the
weaknesses of our old lives. When we pray about it, we say
almost glibly in passing: *"Father, help me put off my old nature
and put on my new nature in Christ."*

The problem with praying that way is that we don't address
the specific issues we may need to put off. It's a weak prayer
because it doesn't require any thoughtful assessment of where
we are in our spiritual growth and process of maturing in
Christ. It's the kind of prayer we can pray on ground level in
our Christian walk, but moving closer to God requires dealing
more directly in prayer with the issues that for us may prevent
the deepest spiritual intimacy.

We all must consider the aspects of our "old nature" that
keep getting in the way of our living the life we desire to live,
and then put them off as Paul instructs us to. But if we really
want to make progress, we shouldn't stop there. We should ask
God to help us put on those opposite positive character traits
that will strengthen us for His life and service, such as:

- Help me to put off pride—and put on humility.
- Help me to put off my critical nature—and put on
  acceptance.
- Help me to put off the coldness of my heart—and put
  on unconditional love.
- Help me to put off worry—and put on trust and peace.
- Help me to put off impatience—and put on patience.
- Help me to put off materialism—and put on con-
  tentment.
- Help me to put off resentment—and put on for-
  giveness.

- Help me to put off my temper—and put on self-control.
- Help me to put off disrespect—and put on regard for others.
- Help me to put off the need to control—and put on willingness to yield.
- Help me to put off lies and exaggerations—and put on truth.

These are simply examples; you'll want to make your own list, as we must make ours. We must all let the Spirit lead us.

Living Sacrifice: Transforming and Renewing Our Minds

The next verse in this passage from Romans continues the thought of presenting ourselves as living sacrifices. It has to do with deliberate decisions on our part: "Do not conform any longer to the pattern of this world, but *be transformed by the renewing of your mind*" (Rom. 12:2a NIV, emphasis added). We're not to conform to the world, but be transformed by the intentional renewing of our minds. We keep coming back to this point of being intentional because that is the way to higher ground. It doesn't just happen—not on any level of our spiritual walk and personal fellowship with God. We must want it, reach for it, and do whatever it takes to get there, knowing we'll face a cost. There is sacrifice involved, sacrifice of self. Something to be given up.

Here the focus is on renewing our minds. This is essential for intimacy with God. It's not just a turning away from sinful thoughts, but a decision to turn our thoughts deliberately toward God, changing the habits of our thought life. We spoke of the importance of choosing to read the Bible daily. That's a vital part of transforming and renewing our minds. God's Word is living and active; the more our minds are exposed to it, the greater the impact.

We also spoke of the significance of beginning to study God's names and attributes, verses and phrases of Scripture that further describe Him. This is something that will enhance not only our personal worship but other types and ways of prayer, including praying without ceasing (1 Thess. 5:17)— prayer that keeps us in the presence of God. The sacrifice of our minds to develop new habits of thought is one of the most significant sacrifices we can make, especially in seeking a closer walk with God.

Dwelling in the Secret Place

As you read the verse below, let us ask you: how do you dwell in the secret place with God? How do you abide under His shadow and find your refuge in Him?

> "He who dwells in the secret place of the Most High shall abide under the shadow of the Almighty. I will say of the Lord, 'He is my refuge and my fortress; My God, in Him I will trust.'" (Ps. 91:1–2 NKJV)

This is a beautiful word picture, but it should be more than that—it's meant to be a reality. It doesn't mean staying in our prayer closet all day, but just the opposite—that we're able to live in the secret place with God in the midst of the busiest of times. We could say it's a matter of the heart, and to a degree it is, but the following verse in the same psalm makes it clear that this is a choice we make: "*If* you make the Most High your dwelling—even the LORD, who is my refuge" (Ps. 91:9 NIV, emphasis added).

We choose to live in the secret place of the Most High if we choose to make the Most High our dwelling—through the relationship of spiritual intimacy. The deeper truth of this psalm is that it's all about our personal relationship with God. We *choose* to live in the secret place with Him *in our minds.* That's where we are aware of our relationship and interaction with God.

We choose to transform and renew our minds with thoughts of God and of His Word. That's how we live, dwell, abide, and draw near to God to consciously focus on Him in our minds. Surrendering our minds to the effort and energy to train them to turn toward Him keeps us in the secret place of His presence. Turning our minds toward Him, we could go about the routines of our day constantly talking to God. It's natural for many of us to do that, but it more often happens only when we have a need and turn to Him for help.

Our ongoing prayers should be more than asking for help; they should include thanksgiving, praise, and worship. We don't need to know God's names to pray that way, but as with our worship, using His names is pleasing and honoring to Him— and it helps build our faith. Directing that focus to a certain name or attribute reminds us that He is our sufficiency in any circumstance.

Lifting the Banner: God of Peace

To dwell in the secret place with God, we begin by lifting the banner of His name: the Lord of Peace. (You will find the following lists of God's names and attributes in the appendix with the verse references.)

Who He Is

God of peace
Lord of peace
Prince of peace
Source of my faith
Our Lord
Our God

What He Is Like

Comforter
Holy
Strong refuge

How He Works in Our Lives

Gives us His peace
Welcomes us into the secret place with Him
Shields us beneath His wings
Calms the storms of life
Is always with us
Will be our resting place
Gives us the mind of Christ

If you have these names and phrases firmly in your mind, you will be ready to use them when you find yourself in a situation needing peace of mind. For illustration, let's assume you are preparing for a difficult meeting with an antagonistic person. You are in the process of gathering up things to take to the meeting, and you're cutting it close on time. If your eyes are not focused on the Lord of peace, your train-of-thought prayer might sound like this one in the midst of your hurry.

Self-Focused Train-of-Thought Prayer

God, I can't believe this is happening, not now, not me . . .
What am I going to do? . . .
How am I going to handle it? . . .
Oh, God, I need You now . . .
I'm counting on You . . .
What if I run out of time? . . .
What if I'm late? . . .
What will they think? . . .

Where is the focus of this prayer? On self. We're told not
to be anxious, not to worry, but this is a prayer based on worry,
filled with anxiety.

If, however, you are dwelling in the secret place with the
Lord of peace, your train-of-thought prayer would sound more
like this one, calm and secure.

God-Focused Train-of-Thought Prayer
(This prayer is reprinted in the appendix as Sample Prayer for Peace.)

Lord,
I'm so grateful that You are the God of peace . . .
You are more than able to give me Your peace, even in the
midst of this situation that has me so upset. . . .
You are the Lord of peace. . . .
my eyes are on You, holy Prince of Peace. . . .
source of my faith. . . .
Help me to believe that You are giving me peace even now,
on my way to this meeting. . . .
You are my Lord and my God who is always with me. . . .
I'm thankful to be in the secret place with You . . .
grateful for the shelter I can find beneath Your wings . . .

for Your strong refuge. . . .
You calm the storms of life. . . .
You are always with me! . . .
I know You are my resting place even now. . . .
Help me to rest in You. . . .
Give me Your mind. . . .

The point is, if we have taken steps to discipline our mind—a surrender of time, effort, and energy—to learn some of the names of God, some of the verses that relate to that part of His nature, we'll be prepared. In crises, the Spirit will bring Scriptures to mind that will be just what we need. How much better it is to be prepared for the crises before we face them!

REFLECTION

Date:_____

To Consider: Think of the chapter you have just read.

What is the one thing that stands out that you might want to incorporate (for the first time or in increasing measure) into your personal prayers? _____

_____

_____

_____

Why do you think this might be important for you? _____

_____

_____

_____

What is the first step you might take? _____

_____

_____

_____

Write a brief prayer, asking for God's help. _____

_____

_____

_____

_____

_____

You may want to add this prayer to your own.

Father, help me to surrender my life to You,
new and fresh every day.
Reveal areas of my heart that I am hanging onto,
perhaps hiding from myself, reluctant to face.
Help me surrender what seem to insignificant things about my life
that may, in fact, be the most important things of all.
Teach me to surrender my mind to You more completely
than I ever have,
to be increasingly intentional about my prayers.
In Jesus' name, amen.

CHAPTER 14

Growing in Supplication through God's Word

When Jesus taught His earliest followers the very basics of what their prayer lives should consist of, His instructions for supplication mentioned only *asking for daily bread*—the essential physical and material needs of life. These "daily bread" prayers come easily to new Christians. But when we look at the prayer He prayed in John 17 and the longer prayers of Paul (Eph. 1:17–19; 3:14–19; Phil. 1:9–11; Col. 1:9–12; 1 Thess. 3:12–13; 2 Thess. 1:11–12), we find they were not merely concerned with daily bread. They were essentially asking God for spiritual growth and maturity, unity, protection from Satan—with not one mention of homes, health, jobs, or provision. They were asking things for disciples in the church that would make them effective in building the kingdom. We encourage you to read these prayers and incorporate them into your own prayers.

If we examine the prayer promises Jesus gave to His eleven disciples who were to build His church (promises for equally committed disciples today), we see that they too are based on accomplishing kingdom business. We summarize them here, along with the two similar promises from the apostle John. From our earlier discussion you'll remember the promises are that we can have whatever we ask in prayer when these conditions are met:

- living obedient, submissive lives in keeping with principles of the Sermon on the Mount (Matt. 7:7)
- having faith in God (Mark 11:22–24)
- praying in agreement, unity of hearts, prayer for the church (Matt. 18:19–20)
- bringing glory to the Father (John 14:12–14)
- abiding in Christ, the Vine (relationship), and bearing fruit (John 15:7–8)
- bearing fruit that will last; love between members in the body of Christ (John 15:16–17)
- asking in the Spirit for the Father's glory and His children's complete joy (John 16:23–24)
- obeying God's commands and doing what pleases Him (1 John 3:21–22)
- asking in agreement with God's will (1 John 5:14–15)

Scripture Prayers of Supplication

Praying prayers that incorporate such principles takes us to higher ground. They represent the deeper truth of petition and intercession because they are totally focused on God's will for His children, His kingdom purpose and glory. When we pray God's Word, we are asking for things that will help us—and those we pray for—align our lives with the heart of God. We'll demonstrate this specifically later in the chapter, but first please consider your own prayer life in terms of the amount of time you typically spend on a daily basis in prayers of supplication. We realize that you probably have your quiet-time prayers as we do, often with prayer lists that help you remember whom to pray for and what their needs are. In addition, perhaps you pray throughout the day when you can. How much time would you estimate you spend daily, on average, in supplication—in your quiet time and during the day?

For our purposes now, let's assume for all of us an average of perhaps fifteen minutes during our quiet time and another fifteen minutes snatched on the run. If you have only thirty minutes a day for prayer, wouldn't you want to invest that time where it would produce sure returns? where you knew the results of your prayers would "avail much" (James 5:16b)? where you would be most led and inspired by the Spirit? where your prayers would be most pleasing to God? Of course you would; we would too.

This is a main reason for praying the Scriptures.

How We Began

When these truths about the reasons for praying God's Word finally caught our attention, we were busy professional people, pursuing secular careers, working long hours, doing our best to grow in the Lord and become people of prayer. Finding adequate time to devote to supplication was a problem, but we managed at least some time each day consistently. We prayed individually and as a couple—usually, at first, for our children (and now, grandchildren), for those in our circle of friends and family, and for each other. These were the people nearest and dearest to us, and we wanted our prayers to make the greatest possible difference in their lives and in ours as well.

During those early years of our walk with the Lord, we were

pursuing our relationship with Him as well as developing a meaningful prayer life, and we now see how the two went hand in hand. The closer we drew to God, the more we sensed His guidance in our prayers. All prayer is the means to the higher ground of *koinonia* (fellowship) with Him, and that includes our supplications. It's when we please and obey God that we are able to draw near, and our prayer lives are a significant part of that. Jesus taught us to pray and said that we should "pray always and not become discouraged" (Luke 18:1). Paul said we're to "pray at all times in the Spirit, . . . with all perseverance and intercession for all the saints" (Eph. 6:18) and to "pray constantly" (1 Thess. 5:17). We're told to come before the throne of grace to ask for what we need (Heb. 4:16), to be watchmen on the wall (Isa. 62:6), to stand in the gap (Ezek. 22:30), to stand our ground (Eph. 6:13), and that we are a royal priesthood (1 Pet. 2:9). We are on higher ground when we pray God's will, coming ever closer to God.

Managing Our Time

Most of us face continuing tension between busy schedules and growing prayer lists (whether these lists are mental or written). Our goal is to take our daily fifteen-minute prayer time and become more efficient and effective at praying God's will through His Scriptures—maybe even praying for more people than we're praying for now.

When we pray for the things that are typically on our hearts for ourselves and others, things like salvation, spiritual growth and maturity, victory over Satan and sin, we are praying for things that will strengthen God's kingdom on earth—praying to draw people into the kingdom and to strengthen those who are already His. So that's where we put our emphasis.

This doesn't mean that we quit praying for the physical and material needs in our lives—James tells us that sometimes we don't have because we don't ask (James 4:2), and Jesus told us to ask for daily bread every day. *But He didn't indicate that God needs a lot of details.* How often have we heard ourselves telling God all about a problem or concern, and then rambling on about the ways we would like for Him to fix it? This is such a natural tendency for all of us that it really requires concentration to change. It's part of the sacrifice of mind—to renew and transform the way we pray requires praying with our mind. We believe it's worth the effort to change.

Let's use Jesus' mother, Mary, as an example. At the wedding in Cana, she saw a material need—the host was out of wine. She went to Jesus with her concern and simply said, "They have no wine" (John 2:3 NKJV). She didn't explain the reasons why there was no wine or the effect it would have on the celebration or the family's reputation or any of that. She didn't point out the water jars as a suggestion for solving the problem. She simply told Him about it and left it in His hands, knowing that He would do something. She said to the servants, "Do whatever He tells you" (John 2:5).

We suggest that the most effective way to increase the weight and value of our prayers to God and for the people for whom we pray is to put the emphasis of our prayer time on things that would build and strengthen God's kingdom, concluded by a prayer like Mary's: They have no wine.

How Would This Work?

When we first began to purposefully learn to pray Scriptures, Kaye wrote some prayers using verses of Scriptures. She began to look at the promises of the Bible and saw that when considered in the context of the passage in which they appear, or in the greater context of the whole body of truth found in the Bible, they have direct or indirect conditions that must be met. When we're living in such a way as to meet the conditions, the promises are there for us. For example, let's look at some of the promises regarding financial needs:

> "This is why I tell you: Don't worry about your life, what you will eat or what you will drink; or about your body, what you will wear. . . . Look at the birds of the sky: they don't sow or reap or gather into barns, yet your heavenly Father feeds them. Aren't you worth more than they? . . . And why do you worry about clothes? Learn how the wildflowers of the field grow: they don't labor or spin thread. . . . If that's how God clothes the grass of the field . . . won't He do much more for you . . . ? . . . *But seek first the kingdom of God and His righteousness, and all these things will be provided for you.*" (Matt. 6:25–26, 28, 30, 33, emphasis added)

> "You have cheated me of the tithes and offerings due to me. . . . Bring all the tithes into the storehouse so there will be enough food in my Temple. If you do," says the Lord Almighty, "I will open the windows of heaven for you. *I will pour out a blessing so great you won't have enough room to take it in!* Try it! Let me prove it to you! Your crops will be abundant, for I will guard them from insects and disease. Your grapes will not shrivel before they are ripe," says the Lord Almighty. (Mal. 3:8b, 10–11 NLT, emphasis added)

"Give, and it will be given to you; a good measure—pressed down, shaken together, and running over—will be poured into your lap. *For with the measure you use, it will be measured back to you.*" (Luke 6:38, emphasis added)

And you, Philippians, know that . . . when I [Paul] left Macedonia, no church shared with me in the matter of giving and receiving except you alone. For even in Thessalonica you sent gifts for my need several times. Not that I seek the gift, but I seek the fruit that is increasing to your account. But I have received everything in full, and I have an abundance. I am fully supplied [with] . . . what you provided— a fragrant offering, a welcome sacrifice, pleasing to God. *And my God will supply all your needs according to His riches in glory in Christ Jesus.* (Phil. 4:15–19, emphasis added)

These are tremendously encouraging promises! But do you see the clear conditions? If we are praying for someone who has a huge financial need—but who is not trying to make God a priority in his life, who is stingy, who has never tithed or given to ministries—can we expect God to meet his needs according to His riches in glory? Maybe. Most likely not. God may be using this very financial trial to get our friend's attention.

What might a better prayer be? A prayer with Scriptures, honoring to the One who has said, "Seek first the kingdom of God and His righteousness, and all these things will be given to you." We pray for our friend that God will be merciful and will help him grow into the kind of man for whom God's financial provision is certain. If God answers that request, our friend will grow into a productive servant of God, and what he gives generously to church and ministries can become loaves and fish in our Lord's hands to advance His kingdom.

Lifting the Banner

Now, let's remember what we discussed in chapter 12 regarding focusing our worship on one facet of God's nature by turning our thoughts to one of His names. This is intentionally lifting our banner bearing a name that will help us focus our minds on that part of who He is, what He's like, and what He does. We worship by the Spirit of God, and when we lift the banner in our minds, He stirs up other related Scriptures to magnify the Lord's name, to help enlarge our view of Him, to build our faith to believe that He is sufficient for any need or concern. Let's apply that now to praying for our friend, lifting the banner of the name Provider.

God identifies Himself as "The Lord Will Provide" in Genesis 22: "Abraham looked up and saw a ram caught by its horns in the thicket. So Abraham went and took the ram and offered it as a burnt offering in place of his son. And Abraham named that place The Lord Will Provide, so today it is said: 'It will be provided on the Lord's mountain'" (Gen. 22:13–14). The Lord provided for Abraham. He gave him a ram to use as a burnt offering in place of his son, Isaac. Remember, now, that context is important. This is the one and only time that God identifies Himself by this name, *Jehovah-Jireh*—"The Lord will Provide."

In this same chapter, we find the following descriptions of the character of Abraham: "'Take your son,' He [God] said, 'your only son Isaac, *whom you love*, go to the land of Moriah, and offer him there as a burnt offering.' . . . Then Abraham said to his young men, 'Stay here with the donkey. The boy and I will go over there *to worship*; then we'll come back to you.' . . . Then He said, 'Do not lay a hand on the boy or do anything to him. For now I know that *you fear God*, since you have not withheld your only son from Me.' . . . 'And all the nations of the earth will be blessed by your offspring *because you have obeyed* My command'" (Gen. 22:2, 5, 12, 18, emphasis added). Abraham was a man who loved the Lord more than even his beloved son, Isaac. He was a man of worship, no matter what the circumstances. He feared God and obeyed Him. This is the character of one to whom God is Provider.

Obedience doesn't mean Abraham was perfect; his recorded life shows that he wasn't. We too can be obedient without being perfect. Obedience includes recognizing and confessing our sins, that we may be forgiven. With that in mind, how strong do you think our prayers would be if we prayed for our friend (or anyone else) that he would become a man who loves the Lord more than anyone or anything in life, that he would worship Him in spirit and in truth, that he would develop a reverent fear of the Lord and live an obedient life? Are these not traits of a maturing Christian? Would not such a person be of value to the kingdom of God, as Abraham was? Here again, we are praying the conditions for blessing.

Sample Prayer for Provision
(This prayer is reprinted in the appendix.)

Now, using these verses about God and some of the principles from the previous verses just referenced (in Matthew, Luke, Philippians, and Genesis), let's pull together a prayer for our friend who has the pressing financial need.

Father,

I come to lift up Your name, to worship You as our Provider. I thank You that You know every hair on John's head, everything about His life—Your eyes are on him. You are our faithful God, the One who provided manna in the desert, water from the rock, clothes that didn't wear out for forty years.

I exalt You as our merciful God, who is kind and compassionate with those in need. Look at John with Your mercy and change His heart. Give him grace to become a generous person, one who is willing to tithe, to give eagerly to ministries, to share with others in need. Increase his faith.

Help him to be a man who loves You more than anyone or anything in life, who worships You in spirit and in truth, who has a reverent fear of You, and who is willing to be obedient.

Father, he is about to lose his home. Please work in his life according to Your kingdom purpose, that Your will can be done in and through him, for I ask in the name of Jesus, my Lord and my King, amen.

Understand, we do not necessarily intend that you use our prayer. Our intent is to demonstrate the principle of using Scripture for supplication, and to change the focus of the prayer from the person in need to the One who can take care of the need.

Focus on God

We like to illustrate praying this way in terms of a triangle. Think of a triangle with three equal sides. Most of our prayers of supplication, if we're not intentional, would look like a triangle—we might begin with God at the point on top, but right away we begin to describe the person and the problem, and then to ask God to do something. The triangle gets broader as we pray about the problem, and toward its base, as we conclude our prayer, we're likely to begin suggesting ways that God might answer—in this case, something like this, "God, help him find a job. Stretch the dollars they have coming in. Make it a better job than he had before, one with benefits, especially good insurance. Don't let them lose their home. They have no place to go . . ."

When we lift the banner and begin to pray God's Word first, we are inverting the triangle. As in our sample Scripture prayer, the base is at the top—that's where we begin, putting our focus on God, His names and attributes, the things He is able to do. As the triangle begins to narrow, we are continuing our Scripture focus by asking for those things that we know are God's will for a person's life and character, which must be very pleasing to Him.

Finally, at the point of the triangle, at the end of our prayers, we present the need: "He is about to lose his home." He has no wine.

Praying for More Than One

Now you may be thinking, if I spend that kind of time praying about every need on my list, I'll never be through! Remember that we are assuming we all spend about fifteen minutes in our quiet time and another fifteen minutes praying on the run. We can maximize the effectiveness of our prayer time in two different ways. Praying prayers from Scripture as we have just illustrated is one way—it has to do with the content of the prayers. The other thing we can easily do is pray such a prayer for a list of names, all of whom have the same essential need.

Here is a practical example. Suppose you arrange your prayers by the types of needs and concerns you'll be praying for, such things as salvation, health, healing, provision, guidance, protection. If you use a spiral notebook or journal, you could designate a page or two for each need and then jot down names and needs (briefly) by topic. As weeks go by, you can add more names to your list, and we're confident that you'll be able to note that some prayers have been answered. You might pray for a different group on different days of the week, or you might pray for each group as you have time, maybe two or three on Monday and none on Tuesday. Don't try to have a legalistic schedule, as it can be self-defeating.

Time is of the essence, and the way we'll save time is to pray our banner-lifting prayer over our list; the Scriptures are appropriate for anyone who is a child of God. If you have a list of various topics as we suggest above, you would pray an intentionally focused prayer over each type need and then quickly go down the list of names and mention each one briefly, personalizing them as needed. Pray for God's will, spiritual growth and maturity, for His purpose and glory, and leave the results in His hands. Simply mention the needs—"they have no wine."

For illustration, we'll use a different prayer, one for those who need guidance.

Sample Prayer for Guidance
(This prayer is reprinted in the appendix.)

Father,

I come to lift up Your name, to worship You as our Wonderful Counselor. I exalt You, Lord Jesus, as the wisdom of God, the One in whom all the treasures of wisdom and knowledge are hidden. Thank You for sending Your Spirit, the Spirit of truth, to live within us. I praise Him as our indwelling Counselor, the anointing who has come to teach us all things, to help us remember all that You, Lord Jesus, have said.

You are our gentle Shepherd who leads us in paths of righteousness, and You have promised that Your sheep will hear Your voice. Help them to hear You clearly saying, "This is the way; walk in it." Help them to be willing to follow You as dependent sheep, keeping their eyes on You. Help them to come apart with You so they can listen as You explain things to them.

I bring these friends before the throne of grace to ask for the wisdom they need to make the right decisions according to Your will and plan and purpose for their lives and Your kingdom:

> *John, who's deciding where to go to college;*
> *Sandra, who doesn't know where to look for work;*
> *Mike, who doesn't know how to approach his boss;*
> *Larry, who needs wisdom in relating to his wife; and*
> *Sheila, who needs to know how to invest the money*
> *her mom left her.*

May Your will be done, for I ask in the name of Jesus, our Shepherd, amen.

The bottom line is: our prayers are stronger, more effective, and more efficient when we put the focus more on God than on the people and the needs we're praying for. We add verses of Scripture that express His will for spiritual growth and maturity, for His purposes that may be far above and beyond simply solving an immediate need. This is the kind of supplication that honors God and pleases Him; and because it does, no matter how slowly or awkwardly we begin, it helps take us to higher ground where we draw closer to Him.

REFLECTION

Date:_____

To Consider: Think of the chapter you have just read.

What is the one thing that stands out that you might want to incorporate (for the first time or in increasing measure) into your personal prayers? _____

_____

_____

_____

Why do you think this might be important for you? _____

_____

_____

_____

What is the first step you might take?_____

_____

_____

_____

Write a brief prayer, asking for God's help. _____

_____

_____

_____

_____

_____

You may want to add this prayer to your own.

*Father, I want my prayers to matter to You
and Your kingdom purposes,
to make a difference in my life and the lives of others,
not only for time but for eternity.
Teach me to pray!
Help me to grow in my understanding and application
of the wonderful promises Jesus left for His disciples;
help me to live in such a way that those promises are mine
so that I can have whatever I ask for in prayer
according to Your will and for Your glory.
In Jesus' name, amen.*

CHAPTER 15

Deeper Cleansing through God's Word

In chapter 6, as part of our initial discussion of the model prayer, we focused briefly on the need to confess our sins daily, asking God to forgive us as we forgive others. May we assume that you have taken this teaching to heart? You've come this far on our journey to higher ground and greater intimacy with God: are you regularly confessing your sins and forgiving others? Are you carrying no resentments or grudges? If all is well in these areas, we want to move on to important matters of deeper cleansing. If all is not well, you might consider finding time to get alone with God and deal with these basic issues. You need to take care of the sins you are aware of before seeking God's view of whatever else you may need to deal with.

Most of us begin our Christian lives with only a general awareness of our sins, usually the more obvious surface sins, things we can learn about each other simply by spending time together. And many of us confess our sins in a vague and general way—"Father, forgive my sins"—at least when we first begin. But as we mature and grow in our understanding of sin, we begin to realize that our sins need to be dealt with individually. So we may begin to confess, "Father, forgive me for my anger." That is, at least, identifying the sin. But better yet, a deeper cleansing comes when we learn to be more specific on a day-to-day basis: "Father, forgive me for being angry with Todd." Finally, we may come to a place of even deeper cleansing when we pray, "Father forgive me for being angry with Todd last night when he was late for dinner. I know he couldn't help it, and he was upset and needed my encouragement." This then, is followed by repentance: "Help me to do better next time. Help me not to let my anger control me. Change me, Father."

The Goal of Confession

This is where our confession is meant to lead—to repentance, a turning away from a sin, a willingness to change in heart, mind, and direction. First we must be aware of our need to change. If we only confess anger in a general way, it doesn't seem so bad. We realize we keep getting angry, but we're not really looking at it as a continuing sin that might limit our going higher with God. Unconfessed willful sin can lead to our holding on to a sin so long that it becomes habitual and ingrained, so automatic that we do it without thinking. This is a sin we are aware of, but we're not willing to address. We keep ignoring it, excusing it, or rationalizing it away. This may not always mean that our prayers will be hindered, but it most likely means that we will not be able to go higher in our level of spiritual intimacy with God, because our God is a holy God who will not be mocked (Lev. 11:44; Gal. 6:7). Why take the chance?

The Higher Ground of Confession

Willful disobedience is not the only thing that can hinder our fellowship with God; a casual attitude toward sin that simply refuses to take a deeper look at sin in our lives can do the same. We may ignore it, but God can see it. How can we safeguard against that?

One way is to ask God to show us the deeper truth of our sins and then give Him the opportunity to probe our hearts with His Word, revealing the truth about our sins: "If we say, 'We have no sin,' we are deceiving ourselves, and the truth is not in us" (1 John 1:8). Then we ask God, through His Spirit, to use His Word to show us anything we may need to see in our hearts. This includes anything that represents what we *should not* do or be (as in the Ten Commandments), or the verses that indicate what we *should* do or be (as in the fruit of the Spirit). We should intentionally read through passages of Scripture that will give Him this opportunity, in addition to our daily devotional reading. What kinds of passages are we talking about? We might begin with one of the following.

- The Ten Commandments (Exod. 20:3–17)
- The Fruit of the Spirit (Gal. 5:22–23a)
- The Sermon on the Mount (Matt. 5–7)
- Children of Light (Eph. 4:17–6:9)

We're not suggesting that you would pray through such passages all in one sitting, but you might take one verse a day. The fruit of the Spirit would be a good beginning.

Because this is a helpful, intentional way to approach searching our hearts and consciences, you might consider keeping up with the verses in these and other passages. Start with one verse or one part of a verse each day in your quiet time. Begin a list of these verses on a page in your journal, and keep adding to your list over the coming weeks, just one per day or each time you use them for prayer. You don't need to write your responses; just record the verses so they will be in a convenient place to review on an ongoing basis. In your daily devotional reading, when you come to a verse that reveals a possible area of sin—now or in the future—add it to your list. Then you simply keep going through the list one verse at a time.

If you have thirty items on your list, you'll have one per day to consider over a month's time. If you are intentional about this and make it a habit, over time your list will grow. Dating each one each time you pray about it will keep you accountable to yourself. When you come to one that is not a problem in your life, offer a prayer of praise and thanksgiving.

Accountability

Where many of us fall short is by failing to hold ourselves accountable for the things we are supposed to be or do. We may do a pretty good job of keeping sin cleared out, but when it comes to identifying the character traits that will increasingly make us more like Christ, we may have little or no means of personal accountability.

The idea here is not to be on a sin hunt, not to focus on the things we are doing wrong or on our failures and shortcomings, but to hold up a standard against which to measure our progress. We'll not be perfect this side of heaven, but we ought to be making progress. We should see victory over some sins in our lives, and there should be clear evidence of Christ-like character developing. If we are willing to put ourselves in a position of allowing God's Spirit to show us these things on a regular basis (and we're willing to deal with them), we can be fairly certain we are not hindering our journey to higher ground or limiting what God might want to do though us. We're not suggesting that this will take a significant amount of time, just a minute or two each day, unless the Spirit has other intentions. It's important to give Him the opportunity.

As we become serious about deeper cleansing, be aware that the more "refined sins" are likely to begin to bother us. These are the sins that lie beneath the surface and are not immediately obvious, things like the motives of our heart. This increased awareness is not a bad thing. Most of us need to deal with things like pride, having a critical spirit, lack of self-control, prayerlessness, worry, and failing to do what we know that we should do. The closer we come to God, the more aware of such sins we will become. That's why Paul could say he was the worst of sinners (1 Tim. 1:15). You'll have your list; we have ours. God will give us all victory if we submit to Him and follow in obedience.

Using Scripture in Confession

In chapter 10 we spoke of praying our way through the Word. We do the same thing when it comes to confession. We pick up the Bible, or our journal list, with prayer: "God show me if this verse reveals a sin in my life that needs to be confessed and repented of." Then we thoughtfully read the verse, or part of a verse, maybe even just a word, and hold it against our lives. For example, if we begin with the fruit of the Spirit, on the first day we might consider the first fruit, "love" (Gal. 5:22a) and ask the Lord questions such as:

> *Father,*
> > *Is there anyone I have not shown love to?*
> > *Is my love unconditional, as I know it should be?*
> > *Is my love for you what it ought to be?*

Do I love you with all my heart?
More than I love anyone else?
More than my husband, wife, children, grandchildren?
What could I do tangibly to show more love for (name)?
How can I tangibly show more love for You?

We're not suggesting that you would ask this many questions about each verse you pray over; we're simply illustrating
the kinds of things the Spirit might bring to mind. Wherever
He leads you is where He wants you to be. As the Spirit leads
you to ask questions, He may bring people or concerns to
mind. Your part is to acknowledge any response He has made.
If He has shown you an area of sin, then ask for His strength
to turn from it, to make amends, to do whatever He shows
you to do.

The difference between a casual Christian who is comfortable with shallow confession of sins and one who has the deeper
view of sin is the willingness to intentionally devote the time
and focus that opens his or her heart to the Spirit. The deeper
view is to be open, to be willing to confess, and to change in
His grace and strength. This is repentance, and it pleases God.
It keeps us moving toward higher ground.

And let's not forget to celebrate the joy of our forgiveness: "If we confess our sins, He is faithful and righteous to
forgive us our sins and to cleanse us from all unrighteousness" (1 John 1:9). We need to reach the place where as we
remember the sins we've been forgiven, we're not discouraged
over what may seem like little progress in this Christian life
we're living—but thrilled that we have such a loving, merciful, forgiving God.

Praying God's Word to Resist Temptation

In chapter 6 we looked at temptation as a test that God allows. We made the point Satan's temptations do not always lead us off into overt sin but are meant to distract us and move us down a path toward God's good in lieu of His best.

There are those of us who are dealing with sin issues that Satan tries to take advantage of. It's far better for us to be pro-active with Scripture prayers and affirmations than to be reactive. For instance, if there is something in your life that you know is a weakness and you are really trying to live in victory, it will be helpful for you to begin collecting Scriptures that will help you be intentional in affirming your position in Christ and God's power for your life. As the apostle Peter instructed: "Therefore, prepare your minds for action; be self-controlled" (1 Pet. 1:13a NIV).

The examples we give here are necessarily general, but if you have an area of weakness, take a determined approach to begin selecting and using appropriate verses as Scripture prayers to bolster those weaknesses. You might want to write them on small cards to take with you to recite and pray whenever you have a moment or are feeling vulnerable to temptation. In time, you will memorize them, and they then can become a part of your prayers without ceasing.

Following some of the guidelines we've already explored, select an appropriate name of God and lift up your banner. Let the Spirit bring to mind the other names, attributes, and verses that you have gathered and learned. If you are alone somewhere during the day—the children are at school, you are alone in an office, or driving by yourself—pray them aloud. This might be a place to begin:

Sample Prayer for Victory over Temptation
(This prayer is reprinted in the appendix.)

Lord,

I lift the banner of Your name, Great High Priest.

I praise You as Jesus, the Son of God, who is able to empathize with my weakness because You have been tempted in every way, yet You did not sin. I approach Your throne of grace with confidence, knowing mercy and grace are there to help me in any time of need.

You are the sure foundation of my life, and I will not be shaken. You are my stronghold, my safe house, the strong tower to which I run! Thank You for the truth that sin is no longer my master—You are my Lord and my Master, my God and my King. You are my Strength!

I rejoice that I have been crucified with You, and You now live in me. You are the Amen to all God's promises—and because You are, I have the strength for anything because You give me power! You are faithful, and You will help me to stand against any temptation. You will show me a way out of temptation so I will not give in to it. You will hold me in Your righteous, victorious right hand!

You are the King of righteousness, and I live and pray in Your name, amen!

This kind of praying is putting our focus on God, who He is, what He is like, what He will do. He will bring us through every temptation. Our part is to give our attention to Him, realizing full well that we cannot hold two thoughts at once. When temptations come, in His strength we intentionally focus our minds on Him.

REFLECTION

Date:_____

To Consider: Think of the chapter you have just read.

What is the one thing that stands out that you might want to incorporate (for the first time or in increasing measure) into your personal prayers?_____

_____

_____

_____

Why do you think this might be important for you? _____

_____

_____

_____

What is the first step you might take?_____

_____

_____

_____

Write a brief prayer, asking for God's help. _____

_____

_____

_____

_____

_____

You may want to add this prayer to your own.

> *Father, if I'm honest with myself and with You*
> *I would rather avoid a deeper look at my sins.*
> *I would rather not hold my life up against the standard of Your*
> *Word. But I realize that a deeper consideration of the*
> *not-so-obvious sins is necessary if I'm to grow in purity and*
> *holiness as I desire to do. Grant me a renewed determination*
> *to face, confess, and turn away from sin, especially the sins*
> *I would rather not acknowledge are there.*
> *In Jesus' name, amen.*

CHAPTER 16

Finding Protection through God's Word

Satan is a reality—the fallen angel Lucifer (Isa. 14:12) who fell like lightning from heaven (Luke 10:18); the one who roams the earth (Job 1:7b) like a roaring lion, looking for someone to devour (1 Pet. 5:8). But rest assured, he is no match for the Lion of the Tribe of Judah (Rev. 5:5).

Deliver Us from the Evil One

Jesus told us to pray daily for deliverance (Matt. 6:13), and He Himself prayed for our protection from the evil one (John 17:15). Therefore we must take the threat of Satan seriously. As we've already pointed out, we have three enemies: the world, the flesh, and the devil—with the biggest threat for most of us coming from the flesh (self). Much of what we deal with is the simple consequence of sin—ours or someone else's. That sin can be caused by the influence of the world, which is under the rule of Satan until Jesus comes again. But though we are in the world (John 17:11b), we are not of the world (John 15:19b); we have been rescued out of the domain of darkness (Col. 1:13a), delivered from the power of darkness

(Col. 1:13a NKJV), and brought into the kingdom of the Son, whom He loves (Col. 1:13b). We are children of the light (Eph. 5:8) who live in the kingdom of light (Col. 1:12), who walk in the light as He Himself is in the light (1 John 1:7a). We need have no fear of the darkness, but we should be alert and wary: "Be sober! Be on the alert! Your adversary the Devil is prowling around like a roaring lion, looking for anyone he can devour. Resist him, firm in the faith" (1 Pet. 5:8–9a).

Submit to God

As we've been focusing on Scripture praying, we already have discussed the importance of our surrender—our submission—to God (chap. 13): "Therefore, submit to God. But resist the Devil, and he will flee from you" (James 4:7). Both Peter and James have said we are to resist the devil, and Paul says we are to stand our ground against him in prayer. Standing our ground in the armor of God, let's keep these verses in mind: "But the Lord is faithful; He will strengthen and guard you from the evil one" (2 Thess. 3:3), and "The One who is in you is greater than the one who is in the world" (1 John 4:4b).

It is the Lord who strengthens and guards us from the evil one. It is the indwelling Spirit who is greater in us than the one who is in the world. We are not standing alone: "Finally, be strengthened by the Lord and by His vast strength" (Eph. 6:10); "O *my Strength,* I watch for you; you, O God, are my fortress" (Ps. 59:9 NIV, emphasis added).

Paul tells us that Jesus is our armor of light—"Let us . . . put on the armor of light . . . put on the Lord Jesus Christ" (Rom. 13:12b, 14a)—and He will help us resist Satan: "Put on the full armor of God so that you can stand against the tactics of the Devil" (Eph. 6:11).

We know that we are children of light, living in the kingdom of light, serving our Lord who is the Light of the world (John 8:12), so this description of the armor seems especially fitting. We gain further insight into the armor when we consider that this passage comes at the end of the letter to the Ephesians. The first three chapters of the letter explain the doctrine of our position "in Christ." The last three chapters have to do with the application—how are we to live in Christ. Paul describes what our lifestyle in Christ should look like as we live as children of light. The armor, then, has much to do with the way we live. We surrender and submit to the Lord, and we resist as we live the life of a child of light, clothed in Christ, our armor of light.

Paul tells us to put on the full armor of God so that we can stand: "For our battle is not against flesh and blood, but against the rulers, against the authorities, against the world powers of this darkness, against the spiritual forces of evil in the heavens. This is why *you must take up the full armor of God, so that you may be able to resist* in the evil day, and having prepared everything, to take your stand" (Eph. 6:12–13, emphasis added). As you read through the verses below, notice that every piece of the armor has a juxtaposed Scripture that shows the names of Jesus as matching each piece of armor—Christ, our armor of light:

> Stand, therefore, with truth like a belt around your waist. (Eph. 6:14a)
> Jesus told him, "I am the way, *the truth,* and the life." (John 14:6a, emphasis added)

> . . . righteousness like armor on your chest. (Eph. 6:14b)
> In those days and at that time I will cause a *Branch of righteousness* to sprout up for David, and He will

administer justice and righteousness in the land.
(Jer. 33:15, emphasis added)

. . . and your feet sandaled with readiness for the gospel of
peace. (Eph. 6:15)
For a child will be born for us, a son will be given to us,
and the government will be on His shoulders. He will
be named Wonderful Counselor, Mighty God, Eternal
Father, *Prince of Peace.* (Isa. 9:6, emphasis added)

In every situation take the shield of faith, and with it you
will be able to extinguish the flaming arrows of the evil
one. (Eph. 6:16)
Look upon *our shield,* O God; look with favor on your
anointed one. (Ps. 84:9 NIV, emphasis added)

Take the helmet of salvation. (Eph. 6:17a)
There is *salvation in no one else,* for there is no other
name under heaven given to people by which we must
be saved. (Acts 4:12, emphasis added)

Lifting the Sword of the Spirit

Paul concludes this passage about the armor with our battle
assignment. We are to take up our sword "and the sword of the
Spirit, which is God's word" (Eph. 6:17b). We've mentioned
in the introduction to part 3 that the Greek word Paul used
for God's "word" is *rhema,* the spoken word. Every verse in the
Bible can be a weapon to defeat Satan, just as Jesus defeated
him in the wilderness. Three times Jesus was confronted by
Satan, and three times He said, "It is written" and then quoted
Scripture: "But He answered, '*It is written*: Man must not live

on bread alone but on every word that comes from the mouth of God.' . . . Jesus told him, '*It is also written*: Do not test the Lord your God.' . . . Then Jesus told him, 'Go away, Satan! For *it is written*: Worship the Lord your God, and serve only Him.' Then the Devil left Him, and immediately angels came and began to serve Him" (Matt. 4:4, 7, 10–11, emphasis added).

Finally, Paul says we who are standing our ground in the full armor of God should take up our sword—and pray: "With every prayer and request, pray at all times in the Spirit, and stay alert in this, with all perseverance and intercession for all the saints" (Eph. 6:18). We release the power of God's Word into the lives of others.

The Battle Is the Lord's

There is a passage that we love that shows how clearly the battle is the Lord's. It's the story of King Jehoshaphat and the people of Judah who heard that a huge enemy army was coming against them. The king called a fast and prayed to God, confessing their helplessness, saying their eyes were on the Lord (2 Chron. 20:1–12). The Lord answered them:

> He said: "Listen, King Jehoshaphat and all who
> live in Judah and Jerusalem! This is what the LORD
> says to you: 'Do not be afraid or discouraged because
> of this vast army. For the battle is not yours, but
> God's. . . . You will not have to fight this battle. Take
> up your positions; stand firm and see the deliverance
> the LORD will give you, O Judah and Jerusalem. Do
> not be afraid; do not be discouraged. Go out to face
> them tomorrow, and the LORD will be with you.'"
> (2 Chron. 20:15, 17 NIV)

Then he [King Jehoshaphat] consulted with the
people and appointed some to sing for the LORD and
some to praise the splendor of His holiness. When
they went out in front of the armed forces, they kept
singing: Give thanks to the LORD, for His faithful
love endures forever. The moment they began their
shouts and praises, the LORD set an ambush . . . and
[their enemies] were defeated. (2 Chron. 20:21–22)

How can you not love a story like this? King Jehoshaphat
sent the choir out in front of the soldiers, leading them out with
praise. The Lord set an ambush, and that was that. This passage
isn't about spiritual warfare, at least not directly. But the principle is one to pay attention to as we are standing our ground
and lifting the sword of the Spirit—we should lead with praise:
"But You are holy, enthroned on the praises of Israel" (Ps. 22:3).
God is actually enthroned on the praises of His people. When
we lift the banner of His name and begin to proclaim the truths
of Scripture in our prayers, our King is present, enthroned on
our prayers of worship and praise.

Trample the Snakes and Scorpions

Jesus gave us another dynamic word picture having to do
with defeating the powers of darkness: "Look, I have given
you the authority to trample on snakes and scorpions and
over all the power of the enemy; nothing will ever harm you"
(Luke 10:19). Snakes and scorpions represent evil spirits. In
Christ and His authority, we trample them. How? The same
way Jesus defeated Satan: It is written, it is written, it is written. We proclaim the Word of God in prayer—Scripture
prayer, focused intentionally on God.

As we consider the prayers we will be praying as we stand our ground and trample the snakes and scorpions, let's take a look at what Scripture tells about Satan that will reveal the character and nature of his demons as well. Let's match that with names of Christ:

Jesus is the creator of all things (Col. 1:16).
> Satan is but a fallen angel (Luke 10:18).

Jesus is Prince of princes (Dan. 8:25).
> Satan is but a prince of this world (John 12:31 NIV).

Jesus is the Lion from the tribe of Judah (Rev. 5:5).
> Satan is but a roaring lion (1 Pet. 5:8b).

Jesus is the Truth (John 14:6).
> Satan is the father of liars (John 8:44).

Jesus is faithful and true (Rev. 19:11).
> Satan is the deceiver (Rev. 20:7–8, 10; 2 Cor. 11:13–15).

Jesus is the One who brings us through every temptation (1 Cor. 10:13).
> Satan is the tempter (Gen. 3:13; Matt. 4:1–11; 1 Thess. 3:5).

Jesus is the One in whom there is no condemnation (Rom. 8:1).
> Satan is our accuser (Rev. 12:10–11).

Jesus is the giver of abundant life (John 10:10).
> Satan is but a thief (Mark 4:14–15).

Jesus is Christ, our life (John 14:6).
    Satan is a murderer (John 8:44).

Jesus is the One who holds everything together (Col. 1:17).
    Satan is a destroyer (Rev. 9:11—
    Abaddon and *Apollyon* mean "Destroyer").

Sample Prayer for Armor of God
(This prayer is reprinted in the appendix.)

So let us rejoice and stand in our armor of light. You can take these verses and lift your banner in many different ways to defeat the evil one as Jesus taught: It is written.

Lord,
    It delights me to come as a child of the light to unfurl the banner of Your name: Jesus!
    It is the name at which one day every knee will bow, in heaven and on the earth and beneath the earth, and every tongue shall confess that Jesus Christ is Lord—including the powers of darkness. I declare it now: Jesus is my Lord!
    I exalt You, Lord Jesus, as Christ my life, the creator of all things, the giver of abundant life, the One who holds all things together.
    You are worthy of my worship, the Lion of the Tribe of Judah, the Prince of princes, the faithful and true. I exalt You as the Truth, the One who brings me through every temptation, the One in whom there is no condemnation.
    It is written—the One in me is greater than he who is in the world. It is written—You are faithful and You will strengthen and guard me from the evil one. It is written—You are my armor of light, the Light of the world.

I clothe myself in You—for You are my belt of truth, the Way, the Truth, and the Life. You are my breastplate of righteousness, the righteous Branch. You are my Prince of peace, the sandals on my feet, the sure foundation of my life, the Rock on which I stand. I take You up as my helmet of salvation, knowing there is no other name by which I am saved. I lift You as my shield of faith, the Anointed One, my shield. And I take up the sword of the Spirit, the spoken Word of God, knowing You are the Word: It is written—in the beginning was the Word and the Word was with God and the Word was God.

I enthrone You on my praise! I proclaim Your name in worship! I come in Your name, King of kings and Lord of lords, amen.

REFLECTION

Date:_____

To Consider: Think of the chapter you have just read.

What is the one thing that stands out that you might want to incorporate (for the first time or in increasing measure) into your personal prayers?_____

_____

_____

_____

Why do you think this might be important for you? _____

_____

_____

_____

What is the first step you might take?_____

_____

_____

_____

Write a brief prayer, asking for God's help. _____

_____

_____

_____

_____

_____

_____

You may want to add this prayer to your own.

> *Father, help me to focus my life and my prayers on You*
> *and on my Lord, Jesus Christ, not on Satan or his evil spirits.*
> *May I live as a child of the light, daily clothing myself in Christ*
> *as my armor of light. Help me to trust that the battles belong to*
> *You—my part is to live the life, wear the full armor, and lift the*
> *sword of prayer! Help me to be faithful to stand my ground in the*
> *strength and power of the Spirit, speaking for Your Word as He*
> *helps me when I don't know what to ask.*
> *In Jesus' name, amen.*

Part 4

A Final Word—
and Godspeed

CHAPTER 17

A Foretaste of Heaven

This life on the higher ground is a preview of what we will experience in eternity.

Is that too bold a statement? Let's consider some things we know to be true (though we may not understand their full dimensions) because they appear in black and white on the pages of the Book we believe. And surely you share this conviction: the fact that we don't understand a thing doesn't make it untrue—or even unbelievable.

Do you understand DNA? or electricity? or where cyberspace is? Some folks have ideas about those things, but most of us just believe them because, in strange ways, our lives depend on them to some degree.

How much more fascinating is it to think of eternity! And of God. And of things that are true about us in relation to those two unfathomable factors in our lives.

Things a Christian Knows without Understanding

Let's just look at a couple of those things.

> For you died, and your life is now hidden with
> Christ in God. When Christ, who is your life,
> appears, then you also will appear with him in glory.
> (Col. 3:3–4 NIV)

> And God raised us up with Christ and seated us
> with him in the heavenly realms in Christ Jesus.
> (Eph. 2:6 NIV)

> I have written these things to you who believe in
> the name of the Son of God, so that you may know
> that you have eternal life. (1 John 5:13)

As we look at these verses, with which we're probably very familiar, we can say that we believe them, and we do. But can we really understand what they say? How can I have died when I'm writing these words at this minute? My "dying" must have another meaning than the one with which I am familiar.

And how can I be seated (present tense) in the heavenly realms in Christ Jesus. I'm right here on earth—or I think I am.

And it is a wondrous thing to know that I have eternal life, but I have to take somebody else's word for it, don't I?

Thinking Things Through—Spiritually

We love the bumper sticker that was circulating a few years ago:

> We are not human beings having a spiritual
> experience. We are spiritual beings having a human
> experience.

Is that a great view of things, or what? When we think that way, we can begin to see biblical truth in eternal terms, rather than try to understand spiritual things with material minds. Are we making sense?

Look at it this way. When we speak of being seated right now in the heavenly realms in Christ Jesus, what we are doing is separating our thought processes from human limitations. Paul's affirmation is about time, or freedom from it. God's view is not limited by time, and He enables us to catch just a glimpse of the way He sees us, our world, and our future with Him— all through the same lens. We can't do that with our limited human grasp, but He has given us His Holy Spirit to open things up a bit.

The exciting thing is that it is the spiritual things that are real—ultimately real. We are actually seated with Christ in the heavenly realms. Though alive, we are dead, and hidden with Christ in God. That is the reality of our lives.

The Higher Ground Is a Preview

Can you let your mind expand its horizons enough to grasp what we've been saying about the higher ground and the deeper truth? We have passed from death to life (Rom. 6:13; 1 John 3:14). We live and believe in Jesus, so we will never die (John 11:26). These are truths because God has spoken them, just as He spoke the worlds into existence (Gen. 1).

What happened is that God became a man in order to satisfy a debt we could not pay, thereby opening the door of heaven for us to walk through with Him. When you responded to the claim of this Man, Jesus, on your life, He took you by the hand and started that journey to your eternal home. The journey is underway, and it has an earthly first leg—step by step, mound by mound, hill by hill—so we can begin, even now, to enjoy the companionship of our Lord. With each step upward, we are one step closer to the relationship for which we were made.

We're in training, in preparation, for what we already possess but cannot see clearly as yet. What we can know, without seeing, is that the hand that is holding and guiding us now—to higher ground here on earth—is the hand that will lead us home.

For all who seek higher ground and deeper truth: "We are asking that you may be filled with the knowledge of His will in all wisdom and spiritual understanding, so that you may walk worthy of the Lord, fully pleasing to Him, bearing fruit in every good work and growing in the knowledge of God. May you be strengthened with all power, according to His glorious might, for all endurance and patience, with joy giving thanks to the Father, who has enabled you to share in the saints' inheritance in the light. He has rescued us from the domain of darkness and transferred us into the kingdom of the Son He loves, in whom we have redemption, the forgiveness of sins" (Col. 1:9–14).

May you be blessed and always encouraged on your continuing journey, and Godspeed!

Appendix

Throughout part 3, Praying God's Word, we have offered the suggestion of lifting the banner of one of God's names in worship, focusing our minds on other similar names, attributes, and verses as prayers of worship and beginning points of prayers of supplication.

We've suggested that it will be helpful for you to think in terms of

- Who God Is
- What He Is Like
- How He Works in Our Lives

In this appendix we have examples of these prayers, along with their related verses and Scripture references. The sample prayers from chapters 11 through 16 are reprinted here. With them we have included two new prayers (for healing and for salvation). All of the prayers are accompanied by lists of the Scriptures referenced in the prayers in the familiar "Who God Is, What He Is Like, and How He Works in Our Lives" format.

Affirming the Relationship

Who God Is

Father (Matt. 6:9).
Creator (Gen. 14:19).
Maker (Job 32:22).
Potter (Isa. 64:8).
Abba Father (Rom. 8:15).

What He Is Like

Love unfailing (Ps. 33:5).
Merciful (Luke 6:36).
Gracious (Exod. 34:6).
Gentle (Matt. 11:29).

How He Works in Our Lives

His hands formed me (Ps. 139:13a NKJV).
His hands knit me together (Ps. 139:13b).
His hands spin me on His potter's wheel (Isa. 64:8).
He sent His Son to die for me (John 3:16).
He has made me His masterpiece (Eph. 2:10 NLT).
He has written my name in His book of life (Phil. 4:3).
He created me for good works that He has planned
    (Eph. 2:10).
He has a plan and purpose for my life (Jer. 29:11).
He will fulfill His purpose for me (Ps. 57:2).
He is making me like Christ (Rom. 8:29).
He guards me as the apple of His eye (Ps. 17:8).
He considers me precious and valued in His sight (Isa. 43:4).
He rejoices over me with singing (Zeph. 3:17 NIV).

Sample Prayer for Affirming the Relationship

Father,

   It's a joy to come as Your child, knowing You are my Creator and my Maker. Your hands formed me, knit me together in my mother's womb, and even today, they're spinning me on Your Potter's wheel.

   Thank You for loving me so much that You sent Your only Son to die for me. Thank You for Your promise that no one can snatch me out of Your hand; I'm secure in Your grip. It's wonderful to think that You have engraved my name on the palms of Your hands and written it in Your book of life!

   It thrills me to know that You see me as Your masterpiece—even though I can't always see it. You have created me for the good works that You have prepared for me to do. I know that even when I don't realize it, You have a plan and purpose for my life. You will fulfill Your purpose for me, no matter how many mistakes I may make along the way. There is comfort in that and in knowing that You are making me like Christ.

   Father, You are full of unfailing love, and mercy, and grace—my gentle, tender, Abba-Father, You are very dear to me.

   You protect me as the apple of Your eye. You see me as precious and valued in Your sight. You rejoice over me with singing—what a marvelous thought!

   I'm so very grateful to belong to You!

Lifting the Banner: Protector

Who He Is

Protector (Ps. 121:3).

Defender (Prov. 23:11 NIV).

Mighty Warrior (Isa. 10:13).

Commander of the army of the Lord (Josh. 5:14).

Strong and mighty God (Ps. 24:8).

Wall of fire (Zech. 2:5).

What He Is Like

Ever-present help in trouble (Ps. 46:1 NIV).

Almighty (Gen. 17:1).

Faithful (Ps. 59:17).

Trustworthy (Ps. 31:14).

How He Works in Our Lives

Keeps us (Jude 1).

Watches over us (Job 34:29).

Guards us from behind (Isa. 52:12).

Goes before us (Ps. 52:12).

Shelters us beneath His wings (Ps. 61:4).

Holds us with His victorious right hand (Isa. 41:10 NLT).

Sample Prayer for Worshipping Our Protector

Father,

I come to worship You, lifting high Your name as my Protector. I exalt You as my Defender, my mighty Warrior, the Commander of the armies of heaven, strong and mighty God, my ever-present help in times of danger. I rejoice in Your faithfulness, knowing You are my keeper who watches over me. You are trustworthy, and I can count on You to go before me and to guard me from behind.

I magnify Your name as the wall of fire around me, as the One who shelters me beneath Your wings, who holds me by Your victorious right hand. With You as my protector, I have no reason to be fearful or afraid!

I worship You in Jesus' name, amen.

Lifting the Banner: God of Peace

Who He Is

God of peace (Rom. 15:33).

Lord of peace (2 Thess. 3:16).

Prince of peace (Isa. 9:6).

Source of my faith (Heb. 12:2).

Our Lord (John 20:28).

Our God (John 20:28).

What He Is Like

Comforter (Jer. 8:18 NIV).

Holy (Ps. 99:9).

Strong refuge (Ps. 71:7).

How He Works in Our Lives

Gives us His peace (2 Thess. 3:16).

Welcomes us into the secret place with Him (Ps. 91:1 NKJV).

Shields us beneath His wings (Ps. 91:4 NLT).

Calms the storms of life (Luke 8:24).

Always is with us (Matt. 28:20).

Will be our resting place (Jer. 50:6).

Gives us the mind of Christ (1 Cor. 2:16b).

Sample Prayer for Peace

Lord,

I'm so grateful that You are the God of peace. You are more than able to give me Your peace, even in the midst of this situation that has me so upset.

You are the Lord of peace; and my eyes are on You—my holy Prince of Peace, source of my faith. Help me to believe that You are giving me peace even now, as I face these circumstances.

You are my Lord and my God who is always with me. I'm thankful to be in the secret place with You, and grateful for the shelter I can find beneath Your wings. You are my strong refuge. You calm the storms of life, and You are always with me!

I know You are my resting place, even now. Help me to rest in You. Give me Your mind, that I may have the mind of Christ and be done with anxious thoughts.

I ask in Your name that is above every name, amen.

Lifting the Banner: Our Provider

Who He Is

"The LORD Will Provide" (Gen. 22:14).

Jesus (Matt. 1:21).

Our Lord (1 Cor. 1:2).

Our King (John 12:15).

What He Is Like

Faithful (1 Cor. 1:9).

Merciful (Jonah 4:2).

Kind (Rom. 11:22).

Compassionate (James 5:11).

How He Works in Our Lives

Knows the number of hairs on our head (Matt. 10:30).

Knows everything about our lives (1 John 3:20).

Eyes are on us (Prov. 5:21).

Provided manna in the desert (Exod. 16:31).

Brought water from the rock (Num. 20:11).

Gave His people clothes that didn't wear out for forty years
(Neh. 9:21).

Changes hearts (Prov. 21:1).

Gives grace (2 Cor. 12:9).

Gives us faith (Eph. 2:8).

Sample Prayer for Provision

Father,

I come to lift up Your name, to worship You as our Provider. I thank You that You know every hair on John's head, everything about His life—Your eyes are on him. You are our faithful God, the One who provided manna in the desert, water from the rock, clothes that didn't wear out for forty years.

I exalt You as our merciful God, who is kind and compassionate with those in need. Look at John with Your mercy, and change His heart. Give him grace to become a generous person, one who is willing to tithe, to give eagerly to ministries, to share with others in need. Increase his faith.

Help him to be a man who loves You more than anyone or anything in life, who worships You in spirit and in truth, who has a reverent fear of You and is willing to be obedient.

Father, he is about to lose his home. Please work in his life according to Your kingdom purpose, that Your will can be done in and through him, for I ask in the name of Jesus, my Lord and my King, amen.

Lifting the Banner: Our Wonderful Counselor

Who He Is

Wonderful Counselor (Isa. 9:6).

Lord Jesus (Acts 8:16).

Wisdom of God (1 Cor. 1:24).

Holy Spirit (John 20:22).

Spirit of Truth (John 14:17).

Counselor (John 14:16).

Shepherd (Ps. 23:1).

What He Is Like

Treasures of wisdom and knowledge (Col. 2:3).

Gentle (2 Cor. 10:1).

How He Works in Our Lives

Teaches us all things (John 14:26).

Helps us remember all that Jesus said (John 14:26).

Leads us in paths of righteousness (Ps. 23:3 NIV).

Helps us hear His voice (John 10:2–4).

Speaks to us (Isa. 30:21 NIV).

Explains things to us (Mark 4:34).

Sample Prayer for Guidance

Father,

I come to lift up Your name, to worship You as our Wonderful Counselor. I exalt You, Lord Jesus, as the wisdom of God, the One in whom all the treasures of wisdom and knowledge are hidden. Thank You for sending Your Spirit, the Spirit of truth, to live within us. I praise Him as our indwelling Counselor, the anointing who has come to teach us all things, to help us remember all that You, Lord Jesus, have said.

You are our gentle Shepherd who leads us in paths of righteousness, and You have promised that Your sheep will hear Your voice. Help them to hear You clearly saying, "This is the way; walk in it." Help them to be willing to follow You as dependent sheep, keeping their eyes on You. Help them to come apart with You so they can listen as You explain things to them.

I bring these friends before the throne of grace to ask for the wisdom they need to make the right decisions according to Your will and plan and purpose for their lives and Your kingdom:

> *John, who's deciding where to go to college;*
> *Sandra, who doesn't know where to look for work;*
> *Mike, who doesn't know how to approach his boss;*
> *Larry, who needs wisdom in relating to his wife; and*
> *Sheila, who needs to know how to invest the money*
>> *her mom left her.*

May Your will be done, for I ask in the name of Jesus, our Shepherd, amen.

Lifting the Banner: Great High Priest

Who He Is

Great High Priest (Heb. 4:14).

Son of God (Matt. 14:33).

Lord (Rom. 7:25).

Master (Eph. 6:9).

God (Gen. 17:7).

King (Acts 17:7).

Strength (Hab. 3:19).

Amen (Rev. 3:14).

King of righteousness (Heb. 7:2).

What He Is Like

Foundation of our lives (Isa. 28:16).

Stronghold (Ps. 27:1).

Safe house (Joel 3:16 MSG).

Strong tower (Ps. 61:3).

Lives in us (John 17:23).

Faithful (Ps. 59:10).

How He Works in Our Lives

Gives us mercy in times of need (Heb. 4:16 NIV).

Grants us grace in times of need (Heb. 4:16 NIV).

Freed me from the power of sin (Rom. 6:18).

Gives us strength for anything (Phil. 4:13).

Grants us power (Ps. 68:35).

Helps us stand against temptation (1 Cor. 10:13).

Shows us the way out of temptation (1 Cor. 10:13).

Holds us in His victorious right hand (Isa. 41:10 NLT).

Sample Prayer for Victory over Temptation

Lord,

I lift the banner of Your name, Great High Priest.

I praise You as Jesus, the Son of God, who is able to empathize with my weakness because You have been tempted in every way, yet You did not sin. I approach Your throne of grace with confidence, knowing mercy and grace are there to help me in any time of need.

You are the sure foundation of my life, and I will not be shaken. You are my stronghold, my safe house, the strong tower to which I run! Thank You for the truth that sin is no longer my master—You are my Lord and my Master, my God and my King. You are my Strength!

I rejoice that I have been crucified with You, and You now live in me. You are the Amen to all God's promises—and because You are, I have the strength for anything because You give me power! You are faithful, and You will help me to stand against any temptation. You will show me a way out of temptation so I will not give in to it. You will hold me in Your righteous, victorious right hand!

You are the King of righteousness, and I live and pray in Your name, amen!

Lifting the Banner: Jesus

Who He Is

Creator of all things (Col. 1:16).

Lion from the tribe of Judah (Rev. 5:5).

Prince of princes (Dan. 8:25).

Way, Truth, Life (John 14:6).

Righteous Branch (Jer. 23:5).

Prince of peace (Isa. 9:6).

Sure foundation (Isa. 28:16).

Anointed One, Our Shield (Ps. 84:9).

Word of God (John 1:1; Rev. 19:13).

King of kings (Rev. 19:16).

Lord of lords (Rev. 17:14).

What He Is Like

Does not condemn us (Rom. 8:1).

Gives us abundant life (John 10:10).

Holds everything together (Col. 1:17).

Faithful and True (Rev. 19:11).

Armor of light (Rom. 13:12).

Rock on which we stand (Matt. 7:24).

Helmet of salvation (Eph. 6:17).

How He Works in Our Lives

Made us children of light (Eph. 5:8).

Brings us through every temptation (1 Cor. 10:13).

Is our belt of truth (Eph. 6:14).

Is our breastplate of righteousness (Eph. 6:14).

Is the sandals on our feet (Eph. 6:15).

Saved by His name (Acts 4:12).

Is our shield of faith (Eph. 6:16).

Sample Prayer for Armor of God

Lord,

It delights me to come as a child of the light to lift the banner of Your name: Jesus!

It is the name at which one day every knee will bow, in heaven and on the earth and beneath the earth, and every tongue shall confess Jesus Christ is Lord—including the powers of darkness. I declare it now: Jesus is my Lord!

I exalt You, Lord Jesus, as Christ my life, the creator of all things, the giver of abundant life, the One who holds all things together.

You are worthy of my worship, the Lion of the Tribe of Judah, the Prince of princes, the faithful and true. I exalt You as the truth, the One who brings me through every temptation, the One in whom there is no condemnation.

It is written—You are my armor of light. I clothe myself in You—for You are my belt of truth, the Way, the Truth, and the Life. You are my breastplate of righteousness, the righteous Branch. You are my Prince of peace, the sandals on my feet, the sure foundation of my life, the Rock on which I stand. I take You up as my helmet of salvation, knowing there is no other name by which I am saved. I lift You as my shield of faith, the Anointed One, my shield. And I take up the sword of the Spirit, the spoken Word of God, knowing You are the Word: It is written—in the beginning was the Word and the Word was with God and the Word was God.

I come in Your name, King of kings and Lord of lords, amen.

Lifting the Banner: Healer

Who He Is

The Lord who heals us (Exod. 15:26).

The Lord God for whom nothing is too difficult (Jer. 32:17).

God of hope (Rom. 15:13).

Our Life (John 14:6).

Balm of Gilead (Jer. 8:22).

Our Helper (Heb. 13:6).

Our Scepter (Num. 24:17 NKJV).

What He Is Like

Our all in all (1 Cor. 15:28).

Sun of righteousness with healing in His wings (Mal. 4:2).

How He Works in Our Lives

Our lives are in His hands (Ps. 31:15).

Fills us with joy and peace (Rom. 15:13).

Never forsakes us (Heb. 13:5).

Never leaves us (Heb. 13:5).

Gives us everything we need (2 Pet. 1:3 NIV).

Speaks and we are healed (Matt. 8:8).

Heals all our diseases (Ps. 103:3).

Loves us with unfailing love (Ps. 6:4 NIV).

Kindness is unfailing (1 Sam. 20:14 NIV).

Looks upon us with compassion (Mark 1:41).

Ordains our days (Ps. 139:16).

Sets a race before us (Heb. 12:1).

Gives us grace (Ps. 84:11).

Gives us strength (Isa. 40:29).

Helps us finish strong (1 Cor. 9:24).

Gives us good things (Matt. 7:11).

Sample Prayer for Healing

Lord,

I worship You as the Lord Who heals us, our God for whom nothing is too difficult.

Our lives are in Your hands.

I exalt You as our God of hope who fills us with all joy and peace as we trust in You, as our Lord who will never leave us, never forsake us. You are our all in all; You give us everything we need; You are our Life.

I praise You as the Balm of Gilead, as the sun of righteousness with healing in Your wings, as one whose authority brings healing. I exalt You as our Lord who heals all our diseases, who loves us with unfailing love, whose kindness is unfailing. Thank You for the compassion that led You to heal so many when You walked the earth, and for not refusing any who asked. I praise You that our days are ordained.

I worship You as our helper, our all in all. Help these I pray for to complete the race You have set before them; grant them Your grace and strength that they may finish strong.

I come in the name of the Lord Jesus, the Scepter through whom we receive Your favor, and ask for the greatest healing Your kingdom purpose will allow—for greatest good and Your greatest glory in the lives of these for whom I pray, amen.

Lifting the Banner: Savior

Who He Is

Savior (Titus 1:4).

Redeemer (Isa. 60:16).

Sacrifice for our sins (1 John 2:2 NIV).

Son of Man (Matt. 26:2).

Lord of glory (1 Cor. 2:8).

Lamb of God (John 1:29).

Good Shepherd (John 10:11).

Way, the Truth, the Life (John 14:6).

Resurrection and the Life (John 11:25).

Lord of the Harvest (Matt. 9:38).

True Light (John 1:9).

What He Is Like

Gave His one and only Son (John 3:16).

Laid down His life for His sheep (John 10:11).

Doesn't want any to perish (2 Pet. 3:9).

Wants all to come to repentance (2 Pet. 3:9).

Wants everyone to be saved (1 Tim. 2:4).

How He Works in Our Lives

Gave His life once for all (Heb. 9:26 NIV).

Was crucified for us (1 Cor. 2:8).

Died for the sins of the whole world (1 John 2:2).

Died that we may have eternal life (John 3:16).

Gives us to His Son (John 6:37).

Sample Prayer for Salvation

Lord Jesus,

I love and worship You as Savior and Redeemer. I exalt You as the one and only sacrifice for the sins of all mankind, as the Son of Man who was crucified for us for the Father's glory. I extol You as the Lord of Glory who so willingly was crucified for us, who died once for all, as the Lamb of God who takes away the sin of the world.

Thank You, Father, for sending Your Son that we would not perish but have eternal life. I praise You, Good Shepherd, for laying down Your life for Your sheep. I magnify You as the Way, the Truth, and the Life—no one can come to the Father except through You. I revere You as the Resurrection and the Life.

I worship You as the Lord of the harvest, as the True Light who came that everyone might see. Father, give these I pray for to Your Son—You do not want any to perish but all to come to repentance. You want all men to be saved. May it be so for these for whom I pray.

In Jesus' name, amen.

Notes

Chapter 4: The Prayer Process

1. Rosalind Rinker, *Prayer: Conversing with God* (Grand Rapids, MI: Zondervan, 1970), 23.

2. Walter Wangerin Jr., *Whole Prayer* (Grand Rapids, MI: Zondervan, 1998), 27.

3. Dallas Willard, *Hearing God* (Downers Grove, IL: Intervarsity Press, 1999), 35.

Chapter 7: Two Prayer Parables

1. The Wycliffe Bible Commentary, electronic database (Moody Press, copyright © 1962).

2. Andrew Murray, *The Ministry of Intercession* (Springdale, PA, 1982), 32.

Chapter 9: Intentional Prayer

1. O. Hallesby, *Prayer* (London: Hodder and Stoughton, 1936), 34.